DATE DUE

JE 9 '04			
JE 16 06			

DEMCO 38-296

*Black American Women
in Olympic Track and Field*

Black American Women in Olympic Track and Field

A Complete Illustrated Reference

by
Michael D. Davis

McFarland & Company, Inc., Publishers
Jefferson, North Carolina, and London

British Library Cataloguing-in-Publication data are available

Library of Congress Cataloguing-in-Publication Data

Davis, Michael D., 1939–
  Black American women in Olympic track and field : a complete
illustrated reference / by Michael D. Davis.
      p.   cm.
  Includes bibliographical references and index.
  ISBN 0-89950-692-5 (lib. bdg. : 50# acid-free paper) ∞
  1. Women track and field athletes—United States—Biography.
2. Afro-American women athletes—Biography.   3. Olympics—History.
I. Title.
GV697.A1D38   1992
796.42'092'2—dc20   91-50946
[B]   CIP

McFarland & Company, Inc., Publishers
  Box 611, Jefferson, North Carolina 28640

This book is dedicated to the memory of my father, John Preston Davis, who passed me the baton. I have tried to carry it faithfully, across the line to victory.

Contents

Acknowledgments

I would like to acknowledge my debt to the people who made important contributions to *Black American Women in Olympic Track and Field.*

Jack Griffin, former coach of the Frederick, Maryland, Track and Field Club and a former United States Olympic Team track coach, gave me valuable assistance and guidance. Jack is also thanked for a life dedicated to helping young black women live rewarding lives.

Dr. Hardy Franklin, director of the Washington, D.C.'s Martin Luther King, Jr., Library, and his staff are thanked for putting up with me during countless hours of research in that fine facility. The research assistance of the New York Public Library's Schomburg Center for Research in Black Culture and Howard University's Moorland-Spingarn Library is appreciated.

Pat Olkiewicz, of the United States Olympic Committee, gave kind words of encouragement and helped locate rare photographs of early Olympic stars.

Rozan E. Cater and Carol Joy Smith, of Washington, D.C., are thanked for their critiques of the manuscript and making sure I remained a "liberated" male writer by keeping the female viewpoint in proper perspective.

In my book of records, you are all gold medal people.

Michael D. Davis

Nomenclature

The word *black* is currently used for African Americans, and it is used in the present work. The words *Negro* and *colored* are used in direct quotations because several of the interviews for this book were conducted at a time when those words were in popular use.

Introduction

Run Fast; Jump High

In Berlin her shoes were stolen for souvenirs, and she had to escape barefoot into a bus from hordes of admirers who, unable to reach her, pounded with furious enthusiasm on the glass windows to get her to wave. In Cologne, mounted police held back the crowds lining the streets to see her, and in Wuppertal, police dogs were used to keep her from being mobbed by autograph seekers. It was like this all over Europe: Athens, Amsterdam, Rome, London—wherever she went.

All this was happening in the middle of September 1960 to a tall, willowy 20-year-old girl from Clarksville, Tennessee, a member of the U.S. women's Olympic team. She was 5 feet 11 inches tall, weighed 132 pounds, and was a sophomore at Tennessee State University, a black school in Nashville. At the seventeenth Olympic Games in Rome the previous week, she had won three Olympic gold medals, an accomplishment not equaled by any of the other 6,000 athletes from 84 nations who competed there. Her name was Wilma Glodean Rudolph, but her friends called her Skeeter.

For the United States, Wilma's victories were three great gold suns in a pitch-black sky. Before then, U.S. Olympic teams had suffered a series of gloomy defeats. Ever since the 1932 Olympics in Los Angeles, the United States had "owned" the titles to the 100 meters and 200 meters. Outstanding American sprinters like Eddie Toland, Jesse Owens, Harrison Dillard, and others had swept to victory ahead of all challengers in each of the five previous Olympiads. Now, at Rome in 1960, the 100 meters was won by Armin Hary of Germany and the 200 meters by Italy's Livio Berruti, while Ray Norton, the American champion, ran dead last in the finals. And this despite the fact that he had been clocked in faster time than any of the victors.

Even worse luck came in the 400-meter relay where the U.S. team, although leading, was disqualified because the still unlucky Ray Norton handed off the baton outside the passing lane. Then came the defeat of the United States' Hal Connolly, winner of the hammer throw at the Melbourne Olympics in 1956, by Vasily Rudenkov, champion of the Soviet Union. Most humiliating of all was the defeat of John Thomas, the

American high jumper. After jumping more than 7 feet in competition 37 times before he went to Rome, Thomas was believed to be the one American athlete certain to win an Olympic gold medal that year. Instead his medal was bronze for third place. Two Russian jumpers, Robert Shavlakadze and Valery Brumel, took first and second places.

It was against this somber backdrop that Wilma Rudolph gave her brilliant performance. First came the 100 meters. She won it in the unbelievable time of 11 seconds flat, clipping three-tenths of a second off the world record and beating the fleet English champion, Dorothy Hyman, to the tape by more than three yards. Her time was not accepted officially because she ran with a helping wind at her back, but record or no record, her victory spread a tidal wave of joy all over America. Proudly, the *Nashville Banner* ran a one-inch headline across its front page: RUDOLPH SAVES DAY FOR U.S.

Next she won the 200 meters. She set no world record this time. In July at Corpus Christi, Texas, she had set a new world record for that distance. Then she teamed with three other Tennessee State University girls to run the 400-meter relay faster than it had ever been run before. It was another world record and for Wilma her third Olympic gold medal.

Two other women athletes had bettered or equaled this performance, but neither was an American. The spectacular Dutch athlete Fanny Blankers-Koen won four gold medals in the Olympic Games held in London in 1948, and the Australian star Betty Cuthbert won three firsts at Melbourne in 1956. But Wilma's time was faster than either of these champions', and no other American woman had matched her victories before then.

Little wonder that Wilma's Olympic triumphs made her the toast of Rome. One of her teammates, Shirley Crowder, the hurdler, had to be rescued by Italian police from an adoring crowd of Roman children intent upon ripping the brass buttons from her Olympic blazer because they mistook her for Wilma. The Italian press called Wilma *La Perla Nera* (the Black Pearl) and the French, enchanted by the way she seemed to float as she ran, called her *La Gazelle Noire* (the Black Gazelle). Another newspaper dubbed her *La Chattanooga Choo Choo*.

Jesse Owens said it in a nutshell. In his "Olympic Diary," published in *Life* magazine he wrote: "September 8, 1960. Wilma did it today. She won her third gold medal for America." He knew what this meant because 24 years earlier at the Berlin Olympiad, he had won four gold medals.

There was nothing in the world of sports quite like winning an Olympic gold medal in track and field for earlier Olympic athletes. Aside from a beribboned medal, there was nothing to gain of any tangible character.

Unlike the amateur boxer or basketball player on an Olympic team, they had no hope of turning professional because there weren't any professional runners. And it was not until the 1970s that the Amateur Athletic Union (AAU) relaxed its stringent rules and allowed amateur athletes to receive lucrative promotional fees for product endorsements and personal appearances.

Olympic games are a kind of war on the international field of sports. You, the athlete, are engaged in a test of athletic skill with athletes of other nations. The national honor and prestige of your country is in your hands; as a member of your country's Olympic team, you are the champion of all its people.

The sight and sound of an Olympic victory is like the tintinnabulation of bells. To win an Olympic gold medal is to be a national hero. Its glory spreads in ever-widening circles until it suffuses the planet. First there is the roar of the crowd as you cross the finish line ahead of all competitors. You rank first among athletes of the world in your event. You stand the highest upon a podium in the center of a great Olympic stadium, cheered by 100,000 spectators. Your country's flag waves high over the multitude, your national anthem is played, and around your neck an Olympic official places the ribbons of the Olympic gold medal, symbol of an Olympic champion. Millions of your countrymen, learning of your exploits over radio and television, seeing your picture in the newspapers, glow with a deep feeling of national pride.

Overnight you have become the "fastest woman on earth." Your picture has been telegraphed to every continent. There is no corner of the globe that does not know that Wilma Rudolph has won three gold medals for America.

Since 1928 when women first began to participate in the modern Olympic Games, American women have won an impressive number of gold medals. Wilma won three at Rome. Wyomia Tyus won three in two Olympiads, and the great Babe Didrikson won two at Los Angeles in 1932. Elizabeth Robinson, Helen Stephens, Annette Rogers, and Barbara Jones have each won two, but at different Olympiads.

Latter-day stars of the 1970s and 1980s like Valerie Brisco-Hooks, Evelyn Ashford, and sisters-in-law Florence Griffith-Joyner and Jackie Joyner-Kersee have also been outstanding Olympic champions. Black women have led the way for America's pursuit of Olympic gold medals in track and field.

Now nothing could be more irrelevant in the Olympic Games, or indeed in track-and-field meets sponsored by the Amateur Athletic Union of the United States, than the fact of race. Good sportsmanship abounds. Among the athletes as well as the coaches and meet officials (with only a few rare exceptions) race has absolutely no meaning. The simple question is, "How fast do you run, how high or how far do you jump?"

Yet no one can look through the annals of American and Olympic track-and-field events without noticing a predominant number of black women among the record holders. They have been prominent on U.S. national teams and have won an impressive number of victories at both outdoor and indoor national meets sponsored by the Amateur Athletic Union.

What makes black women run? Certainly it is not any physical characteristic attributable to race. In 1936, when Adolph Hitler refused to acknowledge Olympic champion Jesse Owens, *Die Angriff,* the German racist newspaper and other publications that supported Hitler's strident quest for Nordic supremacy, claimed black sprinters and jumpers had undergone special operations on their feet to enhance their athletic ability. Others asserted that a black athlete's Achilles tendon was longer, the body temperature higher, and the gluteal muscles better adapted to swift starts. All of these canards have since been proven false by scientists. Television sports commentator Jimmy the Greek was fired when he publicly implied that the biological makeup of black athletes gave them an advantage over white competitors. Indeed, Olympic stars have been of all types.

At Rome, the quartet of women who ran on the world record breaking U.S. team in the 400-meter relay could hardly have been more different from one another. Martha B. Hudson, who ran the first leg, was a diminutive little girl, barely 5 feet. Wilma Rudolph, who ran anchor, was almost a foot taller. The other women were in between.

What makes black women run is a paradoxical question. But so, for that matter, is any question about women's track in the United States. Women's track has never rated very high on the American applause meter. Newspapers and other media give it scant attention except at Olympics time. Before the Rome Olympics one American sportswriter delivered the following jeremiad:

> In contrast with our men's program, women's track and field in this country is in such a sorry state that our former 800-meter champ says: "Oh honestly, I could just sit down and cry when I think about it."
> Nevertheless, we can expect some bright moments. New world record breaker Wilma Rudolph could furnish the closest competition for Australia's pretty Betty Cuthbert. Miss Cuthbert, a triple winner in 1956, is again favored to take the 100, the 200 and with her teammates, the 400-meter relay.

The writer was only one among a long line of commentators who had characterized the American women as "cream puffs" in 1952 and 1956, and had earlier poked fun at them by referring to them as "lantern-jawed muscle queens who look like men."

And America's female athletes have had other obstacles to overcome. There are all sorts of taboos in women's track and all sorts of old wives' tales. The coach of a girls' team has to overcome parental fears that their daughters will be injured or that they will become tomboys. Women's clubs, YWCAs, Girl Scouts, and 4-H Clubs, although ideally suited as potential sponsors, have contributed little if anything to the development of women's track in America.

The public disapproves of female athletes getting rubdowns from male trainers. Women trainers are used by U.S. teams, and always there is a chaperone. The fact is many female athletes prefer getting rubdowns from a man simply because he has more strength in his hands than a woman. Then there is the old saw that athletics will prevent a runner from having children later in life. Wilma Rudolph, Valerie Brisco-Hooks, and Evelyn Ashford are only three of a great many women athletes to have children.

It would be a mistake to assume that the value most black Americans place on women's track is any higher than that placed on it by other Americans. Of course, their chests swell with pride at the thought of Wilma Rudolph and Florence Griffith-Joyner setting world records and winning gold medals, but few people knew Wilma Rudolph existed before the Rome Olympics. After Rome, she was a celebrity. She was greeted with a summer snowstorm of ticker tape as she rode up Broadway with New York's mayor Robert Wagner. Her picture was taken with other black notables—Roy Wilkins, Jackie Robinson, and Lena Horne. She was awarded the Star of Malta at the prestigious Philadelphia Cotillion, the premier social event of Philadelphia's black high society. But all of this came after Rome.

In simple truth, most black women who have distinguished themselves in track and field have had little in common with America's black middle class. If there is a single common denominator for all of them, it is hard, aching poverty, so much so that at the height of her popularity in Rome, Wilma Rudolph did not have three coins of her own to throw into the Trevi Fountain or to buy souvenirs.

What makes them run? Track is the one sport which requires no expensive equipment: no tennis rackets, golf clubs, or memberships in exclusive clubs. Sometimes not even a pair of sneakers is needed. In fact, one of the greatest American women sprinters, Isabel Daniels, won her first race in competition at Tuskegee Institute running barefoot. Track and field is the one sport where a girl by her single effort at running, jumping, or throwing can establish her superiority over all competitors, and if she is good enough, travel all over the world representing her country. In what other field of human endeavor can this happen to a poor black woman today?

Perhaps Earlene Brown—one of America's true Olympians—comes closest to giving us some insight into what it is that makes black athletes run so fast and jump so high. In 1964 she said:

I'm just wondering if this isn't the story of the Negro girls in the Olympics: They pulled themselves up beyond where they really were supposed to be. None of them were supposed to be at London, Helsinki, Melbourne, Rome or Tokyo; or riding first class on a jet plane, eating a five-course dinner and drinking champagne.

They are all Cinderella girls. They come back home and at 12 o'clock their carriage turns to a pumpkin and they have bills, bills, bills. They are the ones who are holding up the high standards of American athletics, the ones all America cheers. But how many people realize just how it really is?

For three generations black women have played a leading role in Olympic track and field events, the premier contests in international competition. This is the story of America's black women in the Olympics.

Olympic Checklist

Los Angeles—1932

Louise Stokes, the "Malden (Massachusetts) Meteor," and Tidye Pickett were the first black American women to qualify for a U.S. Olympic track team. At a 1932 trial meet in Evanston, Illinois, they were designated to be team members on the U.S. 400-meter relay team. At the 1932 Olympics in Los Angeles the coaches, in a controversial and unexplained decision, replaced Stokes and Pickett with two white runners whom Stokes and Pickett had beaten in time trials.

Berlin—1936

Louise Stokes qualified to represent the United States in the 400-meter relay. But again, United States coaches replaced her with a white contestant. Tidye Pickett competed, struck a hurdle in the semifinal event and was eliminated.

Note: Olympics were not held in 1940 or 1944

London—1948

Athlete	Event	Place	Time or Distance
Alice Coachman	High jump	1st	5' 6½"
Emma Reed	High jump	--	--
Mabel Walker	High jump	--	--
Audrey Patterson	200-m dash	3rd	25.2 sec.
Mae Faggs	200-m dash	--	--
Nell Jackson	200-m dash	--	--
Theresa Manuel	80-m hurdles	--	--
Bernice Robinson	60-m hurdles	--	--
Lillian Young	60-m hurdles	--	--
Theresa Manuel	Javelin	--	--
U.S. team: Mae Faggs	400-m relay	--	--

1

Athlete	Event	Place	Time or Distance
Nell Jackson			
Evelyn Lawler			
Jean Patton			

Helsinki—1952

Athlete	Event	Place	Time or Distance
Mae Faggs	100-m dash	6th	--
U.S. team:	400-m relay	--	45.9 sec.
Mae Faggs			
Catherine Hardy			
Barbara Jones			
Janet Moreau			
(a white athlete)			

Melbourne—1956

Athlete	Event	Place	Time or Distance
Isabelle Daniels	100-m dash	4th	11.8 sec.
Mae Faggs	100-m dash	--	--
Lucinda Williams	100-m dash	--	--
Wilma Rudolph	200-m dash	--	--
Mae Faggs	200-m dash	--	--
Willye White	Long jump	2nd	19' 11½"
Margaret Matthews	Long jump	--	--
Mildred McDaniel	High jump	1st	5' 9 ¼"
U.S. team:	400-m relay	3rd	44.9 sec.
Mae Faggs			
Margaret Matthews			
Wilma Rudolph			
Isabelle Daniels			
Earlene Brown	Shot put	--	--
Earlene Brown	Discus	--	--

Rome—1960

Athlete	Event	Place	Time or Distance
Wilma Rudolph	100-m dash	1st	11.0 sec.
Barbara Jones	100-m dash	--	11.7 sec.
Lucinda Williams	100-m dash	--	--
Wilma Rudolph	200-m dash	1st	24.0 sec.
Lucinda Williams	200-m dash	--	--
Shirley Crowder	80-m hurdles	--	--
U.S. team:	400-m relay	1st	44.5 sec.
Martha Hudson			
Lucinda Williams			
Barbara Jones			
Wilma Rudolph			
Earlene Brown	Shot put	3rd	53' 10 ¼"
Earlene Brown	Discus	6th	--
Neomia Rodgers	High jump	14th	--
Willye White	Long jump	16th	--

Tokyo—1964

Athlete	Event	Place	Time or Distance
Wyomia Tyus	100-m dash	1st	11.4 sec.
Edith McGuire	100-m dash	2nd	11.6 sec.
Marilyn White	100-m dash	3rd	11.6 sec. (determined by photograph)
Debbie Thompson	100-m dash	--	--
Edith McGuire	200-m dash	1st	23.0 sec.
Rosie Bonds	80-m hurdles	8th	10.6 sec.
Kim Turner	100-m hurdles	2nd	--
U.S. team:	400-m relay	2nd	43.9 sec.
Wyomia Tyus			
Edith McGuire			
Willye White			
Marilyn White			
Eleanor Montgomery	High jump	8th	5' 7¼"
Terrezene Brown	High jump	--	--
Willye White	Long jump	12th	19' 8¼"
Earlene Brown	Shot put	12th	48' 6¼"

Mexico City—1968

Athlete	Event	Place	Time or Distance
Wyomia Tyus	100-m dash	1st	11.0 sec.
Barbara Ferrell	100-m dash	2nd	11.1 sec.
Barbara Ferrell	200-m dash	4th	22.9 sec.
Wyomia Tyus	200-m dash	6th	23.0 sec.
Madeline Manning	800-m run	1st	2:00.9 sec.
Doris Brown	800-m run	5th	2.039 sec.
U.S. team:	400-m relay	1st	42.8 sec.
Wyomia Tyus			
Barbara Ferrell			
Margaret Bailes			
Mildrette Netter			

Munich—1972

Athlete	Event	Place	Time or Distance
Iris Davis	100-m dash	4th	11.32 sec.
Mable Ferguson	400-m run	5th	51.96 sec.
U.S. team:	400-m relay	4th	43.39 sec.
Martha Watson			
Mattiline Render			
Mildrette Netter			
Iris Davis			
U.S. team:	1600-m relay	2nd	3:25.2
Mable Ferguson			
Madeline Manning			
Cheryl Toussaint			
Kathy Hammond			
(a white athlete)			
Gail Fitzgerald	Pentathlon	--	--

Montreal—1976

Athlete	Event	Place	Time or Distance
Evelyn Ashford	100-m dash	5th	11.24 sec.
Chandra Cheeseborough	100-m dash	6th	11.31 sec.
Pam Jiles	200-m dash	--	--

Athlete	Event	Place	Time or Distance
Rosalyn Bryant	400-m run	5th	50.65 sec.
Shelia Ingram	400-m run	6th	59.90 sec.
Debra Sapenter	400-m run	8th	51.66 sec.
U.S. team:	400-m relay	7th	43.35 sec.
Martha Watson			
Evelyn Ashford			
Debra Armstrong			
Chandra Cheese-			
borough			
U.S. team:	1600-m relay	2nd	3:22.81
Debra Sapenter			
Sheila Ingram			
Pamela Jiles			
Rosalyn Bryant			
Gail Fitzgerald	Pentathlon	--	--

Moscow— 1980

The United States boycotted the 1980 Moscow Olympics to protest the Soviet Union's invasion of Afghanistan.

Los Angeles— 1984

Athlete	Event	Place	Time or Distance
Evelyn Ashford	100-m dash	1st	10.97 sec.
Alice Brown	100-m dash	2nd	11.13 sec.
Jeanette Bolden	100-m dash	4th	11.25 sec.
Diane Dixon	100-m dash	--	--
Valerie Brisco-Hooks	200-m dash	1st	21.81 sec.
Florence Griffith-Joyner	200-m dash	2nd	22.04 sec.
Randy Givins	200-m dash	6th	22.36 sec.
Valerie Brisco-Hooks	400-m run	1st	48.83 sec.
Chandra Cheeseborough	400-m run	2nd	49.05 sec.
Lillie Leatherwood	400-m run	3rd	50.25 sec.
LaShon Nedd	400-m run	--	--
U.S. team:	400-m relay	1st	41.65 sec.
Alice Brown			
Jeanette Bolden			

Athlete	Event	Place	Time or Distance
Chandra Cheeseborough			
Evelyn Ashford			
U.S. team:	1600-m relay	1st	3:18.29
Valerie Brisco-Hooks			
Chandra Cheeseborough			
Lillie Leatherwood			
Sheri Howard			
Kim Gallagher	800-m run	2nd	1:58.63
Robin Campbell	800-m run	--	--
Missy Gerald	800-m run	--	--
Benita Fitzgerald-Brown	100-m hurdles	1st	12.84 sec.
Kim Turner	100-m hurdles	2nd	12.88 sec.
Pamela Page	100-m hurdles	8th	13.40 sec.
Judi Brown	400-m hurdles	2nd	55.20 sec.
Angela Thacher	Long jump	4th	22' 3"
Jackie Joyner-Kersee	Long jump	5th	22' 2½"
Jodi Anderson	Long jump	--	--
Carol Lewis	Long jump	9th	21' 1¼"
Jackie Joyner-Kersee	Heptathlon	2nd	6,385 pts.

Seoul, South Korea Olympics—1988

Athlete	Event	Place	Time or Distance
Florence Griffith-Joyner	100-m dash	1st	10.54 sec.
Evelyn Ashford	100-m dash	2nd	10.57 sec.
Florence Griffith-Joyner	200-m dash	1st	21.34 sec.
U.S. team:	400-m relay	1st	41.98
Evelyn Ashford			
Alice Brown			
Sheila Echols			
Florence Griffith-Joyner			
U.S. team:	1600-m relay	2nd	3:15.51
Valerie Brisco-Hooks			
Diane Dixon			

Athlete	Event	Place	Time or Distance
Denean Howard-Hill			
Florence Griffith-Joyner			
Kim Gallagher	800-m run	3rd	1:56.91
Jackie Joyner-Kersee	Long jump	1st	24' 3½"
Jackie Joyner-Kersee	Heptathlon	1st	7,291 pts.

The Athletes

Jodi Anderson

Jodi Anderson participated in the long jump at the 1984 Olympics. She had set an American record of 23 feet in national competition, but she failed to make the finals in Los Angeles. She was also a heptathlon athlete.

Evelyn Ashford

It took Evelyn Ashford eight years of patience, determination, and hard work to learn that gold medals deferred are not necessarily gold medals denied. At the 1976 Olympics in Montreal, Canada, the 19-year-old sprinter, virtually unknown, finished a surprising fifth in the 100 meters. After the games, she returned to California and began a four-year program of strenuous preparation for the 1980 Moscow Olympiad.

Her renewed efforts soon paid dividends. In 1979, as the 1980 Olympics approached, Evelyn stunned spectators at Montreal's World Cup meet. She beat 100-meter world record holder Marlies Göhr (formerly Oelsner) of the German Democratic Republic. For two years, Göhr had been one of the world's best women sprinters and was expected to capture the 100-meter gold medal at the Moscow Olympiad. Because of her victory over Göhr and impressive performances at national meets, Evelyn replaced the East German athlete as heir apparent to the 1980 100-meter Olympic gold medal. "I gained a lot of confidence in 1979," Evelyn said.

But as Evelyn and other American athletes trained for the Moscow Olympiad, the Soviet Union trained its guns on Afghanistan. President Jimmy Carter decided the United States would boycott the Moscow Olympiad to protest the Soviet invasion. Evelyn Ashford was at a Montreal track meet when word of President Carter's decision arrived. Evelyn and Patricia Connolly, her coach, went to a nearby pub and drowned their disappointment in mugs of Canadian ale. Evelyn talked about abandoning track and

Evelyn Ashford sprints towards a gold medal in the 100-meter dash at the 1984 Olympics in Los Angeles, California. AP/Wide World photo.

field. Her dream of an Olympic gold medal had been dashed by her country's political expediency. "He [President Carter] made the decision and that was that," Evelyn told *Ebony* magazine. "We didn't have any say-so.... I was devastated. That was my big chance."

After the Montreal meet, Evelyn ran in the Pepsi Invitational at UCLA. She fell to the hard cinder track during a race and pulled a muscle. She got up and completed the race in the tradition of a true Olympian, but her despondency increased. "I didn't care anymore," she said.

Evelyn spent that summer on a cross-country car trip with her husband,

Ray, to "think things over," and during that time she weighed her future. She decided to enter Cal State, Los Angeles, and study fashion design. And she decided to continue her track career and prepare for the 1984 Olympics. The dream of an Olympic gold medal still lived. "I still had the burning desire to get a gold medal, so I decided to go ahead and try for it again," she told a reporter. "I had felt so dead inside after the boycott that it took until the end of the 1981 indoor season for me to regain my feelings of drive and desire."

Evelyn started training again. The 1981 season was similar to 1979's, the valueless pre–Olympic season that had brought her recognition and American records but no opportunity to win an Olympic gold medal. Rejuvenated in mind and body, Evelyn won the World Cup sprints in 1981. In 1982 she continued to improve her times, and in 1983 she beat Marlies Göhr again.

The burning dream of gold medals and world records was the catalyst for her continued pursuit of athletic excellence. "I don't have a world record, I don't have any gold medals," she said. "Those are the two major things standing out in my mind, and until I achieve them, I won't be happy with myself, and I won't feel I have achieved my goals or my potential."

At the 1984 Olympic trials, Evelyn won a place on the U.S. Women's Olympic Track Team. Now she was living in Los Angeles where she had attended the University of California at Los Angeles (UCLA). It did not matter that Evelyn would not be traveling to an Olympiad in a foreign country. She was content to have her dream of Olympic gold come true under the blue California skies of her hometown in front of friends, family, and neighbors.

The Los Angeles Olympiad was opened on July 28 by President Ronald Reagan with a spectacular display of fireworks at Memorial Coliseum. One hundred forty nations sent 7,800 athletes to compete in sunny southern California's Olympic gold rush. The Games were boycotted by the Soviet Union and some of its allies, tit-for-tat for the United States' boycott of the Moscow Olympiad. It was now the Soviet Union's star athletes' time to sit home and dream of gold medals that might have been.

A year earlier, after losing to Göhr at the World Championship meet in Helsinki, Finland, Evelyn had made a prediction about the 1984 Olympics: "It's going to me or Göhr, and it's going to be me."

She won the long-sought-after gold medal in the 100-meter dash with a new Olympiad record of 10.97 seconds. She had beaten her strongest challengers, the East Germans Marlies Göhr, Marita Kock, and Barbwel Wockel, a two-time Olympic champion in the 200 meters. Running anchor on the United States' 1600-meter relay with teammates Alice Brown, Jeanette Bolden, and Chandra Cheesborough, she won a second gold medal. The deferred gold medal dream was now a reality. The decision she made on the cross-country car trip to continue her track career had been the right one. Her prophecy "It's going to be me" had come true. Seventeen days after the Los Angeles Olympics, Evelyn lowered her world record mark to 10.76 seconds. She was 27.

Evelyn began to enjoy the economic benefits that came with her gold medals. The American Express Company ran full-page color advertisements in national magazines showing Evelyn running barefoot across a California desert. The ad indicated she had been a "card member since 1983." The Mazda Automobile Company paid her a promotional fee to join its track team and become a spokeswoman for the company. She became a reporter for "World Class Woman," a cable television program about female athletes.

Evelyn's father was an air force sergeant, and during her youth she and her brother and three sisters lived the nomadic life of a military family. She was born April 15, 1957, in Shreveport, Louisiana, and by the time she entered high school, the family had moved several times and was now living in Roseville, California, where her father was stationed at nearby McClellan Air Force Base.

Evelyn ran competitively for the first time when she was a high school senior. Her math teacher was impressed with Evelyn's athletic skills and suggested she participate in track. At the local high school she joined the boys' track team because there wasn't one for girls. She beat the school's star football player every time she ran against him in the 50-yard dash. In high school Evelyn gained regional and statewide reputations, and UCLA gave her a track scholarship in 1975. The running she had done as a hobby would now pay for her education.

Evelyn Ashford did not run her races alone. Running beside her was the alter ego of the woman who coached her for ten years, Pat Connolly. Connolly had been an Olympic athlete, and though she had posted noteworthy success in national competition, she had been a track-and-field bridesmaid but never an Olympic gold medal bride. Pat Connolly never received the financial rewards, the international acclaim, or the gold medals that were to be Evelyn's. Some observers believe Pat found gratification in the reflected glory of Evelyn's success, even though she was not coaching her when she won her gold medals in 1984.

Pat and Evelyn met in 1975 on the UCLA campus. Pat, who had been coaching track on a volunteer basis at UCLA since 1973, had recently been hired as the women's track coach. On the first day of track practice, Pat asked Evelyn to run a time trial in the 100 meters. She ran it so fast that Pat thought she had misread her stopwatch. After Evelyn ran it again, Pat told her she had a good chance to make that year's Olympic team. Evelyn didn't believe her. "I thought: This lady's nuts," Evelyn said. But in the summer of 1976 she went to Montreal as a member of the U.S. team.

She ran the 100 meters and finished fifth, one place ahead of the better-known and more experienced American Chandra Cheeseborough and three places ahead of Marlies Göhr, the young East German who was to become Evelyn's toughest rival.

After the Olympics, Pat and Evelyn returned to California, and their relationship became closer. "She was like my mother for a few years," Evelyn told *Ms. Magazine*. "She took my parents' place in my mind and maybe in hers, but after 1980 I kind of woke up. We were still friends but not mother-daughter. I grew up. It was hard for both of us." Pat saw the relationship a little differently. "We weren't really like sisters," Pat said. "And we weren't really like mother and daughter, but if you need to use words to make people understand what we went through, those are the best words."

Pat and Evelyn offered an interesting contrast of personalities. Pat was effusive, outgoing, and dramatic; Evelyn, more reserved and introspective. Evelyn grew up when women in sports were gaining wide acceptance. Pat came along at a time when the femininity of female athletes was often questioned. "If you were an athlete in anything other than synchronized swimming, people figured you were either a lesbian or a tramp," Pat said, remembering her athletic career in the late 1950s.

Pat wanted to protect Evelyn from the pitfalls that had troubled her own career. "You can make your own mistakes," she told Evelyn, "but you can't repeat the ones I have made." Pat was married to Hal Connolly, who had won the gold medal in the hammer throw at the 1956 Olympics. Though Pat had never experienced the splendor of winning an Olympic gold medal, she understood its significance to Evelyn.

Pat Connolly's father died a hero at Pearl Harbor. Her mother remarried when she was 4 and had five children. Her mother was from a Mormon family. Pat learned to cook and sew, and took up ballet. Her driver's education teacher took her to a local track meet and suggested she enter several events. In the long jump she used her ballet training. "I did a *grand jeté* leap and broke the record," she said.

Pat pursued a track-and-field career which distanced her from her strict Mormon upbringing, and went to the 1960 Rome Olympics as a member of the U.S. women's track team. Though she had participated in three Olympiads, she won no gold medals but did develop an interest in helping female runners reach their full potential. Nationally, she had won eight pentathlon championships, and now she wanted to be a track coach. Pat Connolly wanted to help Evelyn Ashford attain the gold-medal dream that had eluded her own career.

Evelyn became disinterested in pursuing her studies, and the athletic scholarship did not pay for books and the other necessities of college life. She dropped out of UCLA in 1979 and went to work in a Nike shoe store.

Pat had agreed to continue to coach her, even though she was no longer a UCLA student. She practiced in the afternoon and worked at the shoe store until eight or nine at night.

Evelyn had to impose a Spartan self-discipline to meet the goals to which she aspired. "I am willing to put in the hours, even though one of the hardest things about running for me is just getting up every morning to train," she told *Track and Field Magazine* in 1981. "Once I'm out on the track, I will work hard, it's just the getting there that's hard."

Evelyn told Pat she thought she needed a different kind of coaching if she was to win in Los Angeles. They were having philosophical differences. Evelyn was turning more toward her husband, Ray Washington, for training and advice. She made the decision to let Ray, who coached men's basketball at Mount San Jacinto Junior College, handle her career. Pat accepted Evelyn's decision with grace and some regret but wished her well in her quest for the gold medal. "Even I can really read Evelyn only 90 percent of the time," Pat said. "The eyes which seem so expressive can be very secretive. She is much more complex than what appears on the surface." When Evelyn won the gold medals, her husband was her coach.

Though Evelyn had finally realized her dream of winning an Olympic gold medal, there was one other deferred dream waiting in the wings: Evelyn and Ray wanted a child. "We both always visualized seeing her win a gold medal," Ray Washington said. "So, that came first. But then the boycott of the 1980 Games came and we had to wait four more years." The birth of Raina Ashly Washington, in May 1985, did not end Evelyn's track career, but it did focus an interesting light on the issue of childbirth and athletics.

The year after Raina's birth, Evelyn ranked first in the world in the 100 meters for the fourth time and ran a 10.88, the best 100-meter time in the world for 1986. In February 1986 she entered the Vitalis Olympic Invitational and won the 55-meter dash in 6.6 seconds. Evelyn Ashford's pregnancy and the subsequent birth of her daughter offered more clues to the long-debated question of whether motherhood and athletic excellence are compatible. Other star performers had given birth at the height of their athletic careers. Wilma Rudolph had a child before winning three gold medals at the 1960 Rome Olympiad. But Rudolph's pregnancy and the out-of-wedlock birth of her daughter Yolanda was not widely publicized.

Fanny Blankers-Koen of the Netherlands was a 30-year-old mother of two children when she won four women's track events—the 100 meters, 200 meters, 80-meter hurdles, and 1600-meter relay—at the London Olympics in 1948. Olympic champions Valerie Brisco-Hooks, Ingrid Kristiansen, and Tatyana Kazankina exceeded their previous best performances after having children.

"Motherhood made me a better runner," Evelyn said. "My endurance was better. I could run a mile, two miles, or four miles and have fantastic times. I could lift the same weight I lifted before I got pregnant. But it did take a while to get the sprinting speed back."

Dr. James Clapp, an obstetrician and gynecologist at the University of Vermont, suggests that Evelyn's statement may be medically accurate. He submits that women's legs may be stronger after pregnancy because they have been carrying an average of 25 pounds additional weight. During pregnancy, he contends, a woman's heart rate and stroke volume rise, increasing the amount of blood the heart pumps. This improves fitness and endurance.

But before Evelyn could reap the athletic benefits of motherhood, she had to shed the 40 pounds she gained while carrying Raina. It was her husband who found a kind way to encourage her to lose weight. "He bought me size five dresses," she said, the size she wore before her pregnancy.

In the spring of 1986, after winning a race at a New Jersey track meet, she sprinted to the stands, picked Raina up, and showed her to the New Jersey fans. Her deferred dream of gold medals and a baby had finally become a reality. The wait had been worthwhile.

In 1988, at the Seoul Olympics, she won two more medals: a gold in the 400-meter relay and a silver in the 100-meter dash. Though most of the media attention focused on Florence Griffith-Joyner and Jackie Joyner-Kersee, Evelyn had joined Wilma Rudolph and Wyomia Tyus as a career triple gold medal winner. She had known the glare of the media spotlight, and now she didn't mind sharing it with others.

Margaret Bailes

Margaret Bailes was a member of the U.S.A.'s 400-meter 1968 relay team that won a gold medal and set Olympic and world records of 42.8 seconds.

Jeanette Bolden

Jeanette Bolden was a 12-year-old student at Compton, California's Sunair School for Asthmatics when she took an interest in track. Ten years later she ran the 60-yard dash in 6.0 seconds, setting a new indoor world record. She was a member of the 1980 U.S. Olympic 400-meter relay team that didn't get to run because of the boycott, but at Los Angeles in 1984 she finished fourth in the 100-meter dash with a time of 11.25 seconds.

Rosie Bonds

Rosie Bonds says the funniest thing she remembers about her track career is winning the 80-meter hurdles at the national AAU outdoor meet in Dayton, Ohio, in 1963. At that time she had been running hurdles only two months. Her coach then, Dennis Ikenberry of the University of California at Riverside, Rosie's hometown, has a film of the race that puts them in stitches whenever they look at it. There is Rosie running up to a hurdle, stopping, jumping over it, then repeating this same pattern with each hurdle, all the while wobbling from left to right as she speeds merrily along.

It was a clumsy, graceless performance, but it was fast enough for her to win over veteran hurdler Jo Ann Terry, who had won a gold medal that year in the 80-meter hurdles at the Pan-American Games in Brazil and was holder of the American women's outdoor record in the 70-meter hurdles.

Within 18 months from the day she won her first hurdles race, Rosie had twice been crowned national outdoor hurdles champion (1963, 1964) and had been chosen to represent the U.S. women's team to the Tokyo Olympic Games. And she had set a new American record in the 80-meter hurdles of 10.8 seconds, equaling the winning time of Irina Press, the Russian hurdler at the Rome Olympics in 1960. That was Rosie Bonds.

There are two sides to the Rosie Bonds coin. No one rose faster; no one fell quicker. The 1963 USSR-U.S. dual meet in Moscow was a bad one for the U.S. team. The American girls lost 10 out of 10 events that year, and everybody was blaming everyone else. The *Amateur Athlete* wrote: "The U.S. women were a distinct disappointment. Here again, the Americans were hurt by officiating, when Rosie Bonds and Sandra Knott were disqualified for false starts in two races. But when Galina Popova upset Edith McGuire in the 100-meter dash and the Soviet relay team edged the Americans, the handwriting was on the wall."

There was a conflict on the American team. Jo Ann Terry said of the coaches: "They tried to stop us from playing cards; they didn't want us to dance; they didn't want us to do things that released tension. They had a meeting until 2 a.m. the night before I was to compete in the hurdles. The next day I went out, tripped on a hurdle, and fell on my face." Jo Ann didn't finish the race.

The night after the meet there was a party. Rosie and Sandra Knott went, but they didn't stay. "I felt no good, sick, sick," said Rosie.

Things got worse in Warsaw. Rosie was disqualified once again for two false starts. The coaches were furious. Rosie could hardly object when they put young Tammie Davis into the race at Braunschweig, Germany. Tammie ran fast enough to set a new American record of 11 seconds. It was small compensation for Rosie to pull herself together in the next meet in London and to win the race in the slower time of 11.1 seconds. The European trip had been disastrous, and Rosie made no small contribution to the results.

Things got better in 1964. She won the national outdoor meet in Hanford, California, in July and this time set a new American record. Then came the Olympic trials at Randalls Island, New York, in August. Five minutes after she came on the track, her running shoes were stolen, and she had to run in borrowed shoes. Once again she ran her race in 10.8 seconds, equaling the time she made at Hanford and coming in first, ahead of Cherrie Sherrard of Oakland, California, and Leaseneth O'Neal, a student from the University of Hawaii.

In the Tokyo Olympiad, Rosie's two companion hurdlers, Cherrie Sherrard and Leaseneth O'Neal, were eliminated in trial heats. Rosie, running with her usual clumsiness, stumbled into the finals. Out of six finalists, she ran last, but even in last place she ran the 80-meter hurdles faster than any other American woman runner ever had, in 10.6 seconds. Her record was not allowed, however, because the judges ruled that she was helped by a favorable wind at her back.

After the Moscow debacle in 1963 Rosie had promised herself that nothing else mattered as much as returning to Moscow and redeeming herself. She was not concerned about Tokyo or the national championship. She had set her sights on returning to Moscow to show the Russians she knew how to hurdle. She was not disheartened by Tokyo, and she was still running strong in 1965. But now she had no coach and didn't belong to a track club. It was Rosie Bonds against the world. Running unattached, she ran the 100-yard dash in 10.7 seconds in May, a very fast time. She ran the 100-meter hurdles in 13.9 seconds, also a fast time. And she made the U.S. team which traveled to Europe in 1965. She was going back to Russia, and then to Warsaw where she had also been disqualified, and finally on to Munich. Jack Griffin, who had been assistant coach in Tokyo, was coach of the team, and Nell Jackson, a member of the 1948 team in London, was manager.

In the Russian meet, held in Kiev's Central Stadium, Rosie was beaten by Irina Press, who ran the 80-meter hurdles in 10.5 seconds. Rosie came in third with a time of 10.9 seconds. It was the fastest time of any American. Then something happened. Rosie's past performance in 1963 caught up with her. The coaches of the 1963 team had warned other coaches about these runners. Discipline seemed lax. After a long banquet, the U.S. team was scheduled to go to bed so they could leave early the next morning for Warsaw. But Rosie was not ready to go to bed, and at bed check she was not there.

Something had to be done to maintain discipline. The coaches made an example of Rosie and sent her home, as the *New York Times* reported, "for a breach of team discipline." Rosie's running days were over.

Americans are quick to forget losers, and today hardly anyone remembers Rosie Bonds. She has not competed since 1965. But before we write Rosie Bonds a ticket to oblivion, we should pause to realize that in 1968, if she had kept training, she would probably have been the United States' best chance for a gold medal at Mexico City. The United States had not won a gold medal in a hurdles event since the victory of Mildred "Babe" Didrikson in Amsterdam in 1932.

Rosie came from a family of athletes. In 1964 one of her brothers was California state high hurdles champion; another held the state championship in the long jump with a leap of 25 feet, 3 inches. A third brother was a professional baseball player. Rosie grew up in a black–Mexican ghetto in Riverside, California. Her father was a plasterer, who made an adequate living for the time, and soon the Bonds family moved out of the slums and into a house of their own. She graduated from Polytechnic High School and attended the Junior College of the University of California at Riverside for nearly two years. That is where she met Dennis Ikenberry. He encouraged her to take training seriously. Early in the morning she began running four to six miles cross-country, regardless of the weather. She worked a full day and then came home for a snack before walking two miles to attend classes from 7:00 to 10:00 P.M. A better-than-average student, she earned an A in chemistry, but when work and training crowded her schedule, her grade dropped to C.

Rosie lived in a black world filled with blind alleys. "The only white people we ever saw," she said, "were our schoolteachers." She looked for answers to questions of race discrimination by reading books about Black Muslims. She identified with characters in Richard Wright's books. Indeed, Rosie could easily have been Bigger Thomas' sister. But she tried reading James Baldwin's *Another Country*, and it left her cold. One day, while she was training for the Tokyo Olympiad, she burst out in deep anger: "Here we are killing ourselves on the track for the United States while they are blowing our heads off with sticks of dynamite," an obvious reference to black girls who had been killed in a bomb blast while attending Sunday school in a Birmingham, Alabama, church.

Whether Baron de Coubertin, founder of the modern Olympic Games, intended it or not, international competition has become a test of national prestige, a kind of war on the sports field. Rosie Bonds was a casualty of that war. But she need not have been if she had been given the coaching, training opportunities, and support other countries give their athletes.

Karin Balzer of Germany, victor of the hurdles in Tokyo, and Irina Press, leading Russian hurdler, both had months of training and coaching before the Olympiad. Not Rosie. She was busy earning a living, going to school, and trying to hold a job in a world where employers did not look with favor on a part-time employee apt to leave on the shortest notice for the Olympic Games or other international competition.

Shortly before the Tokyo Games Rosie was looking for a job. It was an election year, so both candidates for Congress tried to get her to campaign for them in black neighborhoods, not because they wanted to help Rosie but because they thought Rosie's popularity would help them. Finally, a building-trades local union hired her three weeks before she left for Tokyo. The money she earned paid the rent while she was in Japan and bought her a few clothes for the trip. Like most of the other runners on the Olympic team, Rosie came home broke.

Rosie was a prime example of an American woman athlete of great natural ability completely isolated from the opportunity to train adequately.

In 1956 Lyman Bingham, then executive director of the U.S. Olympic Committee, suggested getting women athletes from America's factories and industrial plants. He said:

> It so happens we don't have the means for developing women's teams. High schools and colleges don't go in for women's track. Women's sports are available mostly in industrial plants.
>
> There must be thousands of fine athletes whose talents are buried under a lathe or machine of some sort ... with never an opportunity to come to the top. I hope to see the day when our factories promote track and field. It would be a great boost for our Olympic team.

Valerie Brisco-Hooks

In 1987 Olympic champion Valerie Brisco-Hooks proved what medical experts had known for some time: Aerobic exercise increases the human heart's capacity for a lot of things.

At the Pan-American Games in Indianapolis, Valerie had just won the gold medal in the 1600-meter relay when she was approached by a deaf teenager who had impaired eyesight. The boy asked Valerie if she would pose with him for a picture. She did more than that. She slipped her gold medal around his neck and after the picture was taken smiled and walked

Valerie Brisco-Hooks wins the 400-meter race at Los Angeles' Memorial Coliseum at the 1984 Olympics. Kathryn Cook (center) of Great Britain was second and Chandra Cheeseborough of Jacksonville, Florida, finished third. AP/Wide World photo.

away, leaving the medal with her young admirer. "It's not that the medal didn't mean anything to me," she told a reporter. "I am sure it meant more to him."

That was Valerie Brisco-Hooks' gold-hearted way of showing appreciation for the fame and fortune she had earned three years earlier, by winning three gold medals at the 1984 Olympics in Los Angeles, California.

She entered the 1984 Los Angeles Olympics a virtual unknown and left with three gold medals for the 200 meters, 400 meters, and the 1600-meter sprint relay. At the Olympic Games, Valerie ran nine races in seven days and became the first American athlete, male or female, to capture the 200 and 400 meters titles at the same Olympiad. She won her gold medals two years after giving birth to a son.

Valerie Brisco-Hooks set Olympic and American records in all her finals. She ran the first race, the 400 meters, in an outstanding 48.83 seconds. The 200 meters final saw a performance of 21.81 seconds, and then she ran a 49.23 seconds third leg in the 1600-meter relay, won by the Americans easily in 3 minutes, 18.29 seconds. She was the first American woman since Wilma Rudolph in 1960 to win three gold medals at the same Olympiad. One sportswriter described her as a "thoroughbred of a sprinter, who runs with raw power and with artful grace."

After the 1984 Olympiad, she went to Europe and was beaten by the GDR sprinters in the 200 meters. The European press widely publicized the defeat of the American athlete who had won three gold medals at Los Angeles. They didn't explain, however, that Valerie had passed her peak for that year and that the East German athletes were just reaching theirs. But in August 1985, at the Weltklasse meet in Zurich, Switzerland, she was ready for the Europeans. She beat Marita Koch in the 200 meters and reaffirmed her gold medal credentials.

In 1988, she won a silver medal in Seoul as a member of the second-place 1600-meter relay team

Valerie had natural athletic ability as a teenager and it came without effort. She was an outstanding sprinter at Los Angeles' Locke High School even though she didn't practice very often. "Workouts weren't the thing for me," she told *Women's Sports and Fitness Magazine*. "I'd just jog and go home, and that was it."

Her first noteworthy performance came in 1977 when she was timed in 54.19 seconds for the 400 meters. In 1979, while a high school student, she ran the 400 meters in a surprising 52.08 seconds, which remained her best time in the event until the 1984 Olympic trials.

Valerie Brisco-Hooks was born in Greenwood, Mississippi, on July 6, 1960, the year Wilma Rudolph won an unprecedented three gold medals at the Rome Olympiad. She was the sixth of 10 children of Arguster and Guitherea Brisco. Arguster Brisco moved his family to Los Angeles when Valerie was 5.

In 1974, Valerie's 18-year-old brother Robert was shot to death by a stray bullet while running on the Locke High School track near Watts. She had practiced on that same track, and Robert had been an early inspiration for his sister's track career.

In 1979 Valerie met Bob Kersee, who became her coach when she joined his World Class Track Team. Kersee convinced Valerie that she had what it took to be an Olympic champion but that she would have to train and train hard if she wanted an Olympic gold medal. He told her that lazy athletes do not win gold medals. As a member of the World Class Track Club, she trained with Jackie Joyner-Kersee, Bob Kersee's wife, and Florence Griffith-Joyner. She worked long and hard, often training seven hours a day, five days a week, then lifting weights for two to three hours a day. She would complete these workouts by doing 250 push-ups and 1,000 sit-ups.

She met Alvin Hooks at Cal State, Northridge, in 1979 and two and a half years later they married. They moved to Philadelphia after Alvin

Hooks was drafted by the Philadelphia Eagles football team in 1981 as a wide receiver. But in 1982 he injured his knee, and the team released him. He was picked up and then cut by the United States Football League's Los Angeles Express.

Valerie missed the 1982 track season because of the birth of her son, Alvin Hooks, Jr. She returned to competition in 1983, but first there was this problem of an additional 40 pounds she had gained during her pregnancy. To lose the weight, Valerie wrapped her body in cellophane and ran in place in the bathroom while hot water pouring from the shower created a steamroom.

During the summer of 1984, after separations and attempts at reconciliation, Valerie and Alvin were divorced, but she continued to train. She ended the pre–Olympic season with her best time of 11.39 seconds for the 100 meters and 23.10 seconds for the 200 meters. She was another female athlete who turned in her best performances after having a child.

Unlike most top contenders, she ran in the Athletic Congress (TAC) track meet, held only a week before the U.S. Olympic trials. Most Olympic athletes forego meets scheduled near Olympic trials to avoid injuries that could take them out of trial competition. But at the TAC meet she set a new American record of 49.83 seconds for the 400 meters. A week later, at the Olympic trials, she won the 200 meters with a personal best of 22.16 seconds and improved her 400 meters time with a 49.79 seconds, finishing second behind Chandra Cheeseborough, who set a new American record of 49.28 seconds.

Like several other latter-day stars, Valerie has received her share of commercial endorsements and paid public appearances, which made it possible for her to indulge her penchant for stylish clothes and jewelry. Valerie often wears her hair braided and lets it hang down to the small of her back. She spends a lot of her time serving as a role model for young children. Valerie has narrated and appeared in antidrug public-service films that are used in public schools.

Her track career will be remembered by thousands of fans who enjoyed watching her participate in Olympic and national competition. But her biggest fan will probably always be the spectator who can tell his friends that he has one of Valerie Brisco-Hooks' gold medals.

Alice Brown

At the 1984 Olympics in Los Angeles, California, Alice Brown was a member of the gold medal 400-meter relay team. She won a second place medal in the 100-meter dash. At the 1988 Olympiad she won a gold medal as a member of the 400-meter relay team.

Doris Brown

Doris Brown placed fifth in the 800-meter run at the 1968 Olympics in Mexico City.

Earlene Brown

In the summer of 1964 Earlene Brown was living at 115-15 Athens Way, Los Angeles, California, a fitting address for a 250-pound Amazon who three times had been a member of the U.S. women's Olympic team. Athens Way is some distance from the center of town in a working-class district of Los Angeles. Number 115-15 was a storefront. Probably, unable to develop it as business property, its owner built a cardboard-thin partition straight down the middle and rented it as two apartments. Earlene lived in one half, and a white couple from Arkansas occupied the other. Famous as Earlene was, her white neighbors did not even know her name or that she was the holder of the American's women's record in the shot put and discus.

One hot July morning, Athens Way welcomed some distinguished visitors. Earlene brought them racing up the Los Angeles freeway in a car borrowed from a friend. She stopped in front of her home, and out stepped three of the Soviet Union's most famous women athletes: Tamara Press, holder of the world record in shot put and discus; Galina Zybina, shot-putter; and Yevgeniya Kuznetsova, discus thrower. The day before they had competed in a dual meet between the United States and Russia.

Soviet-American cultural and sports affairs are governed by strict protocol, but it is doubtful the State Department ever planned or even knew about Earlene's junket with her Russian friends. Gavril Korobkov, head coach of the Russian team, let Earlene kidnap his stars. Earlene was an old friend of the Russians. She had taught them to "rock and roll" and "cha-cha" in Melbourne, competed against them and fraternized with them in Moscow, Rome, Philadelphia, and Los Angeles. She was a gallant competitor, a trusted friend. So Korobkov let Earlene carry off his athletes even though she spoke no Russian and the Soviet athletes could not speak a word of English. He might not have been so willing to let them go had he known how rickety was the car Earlene had borrowed, how fast she drove, or what the Los Angeles Freeway was like.

Across the street from Earlene's apartment was the Free Will Missionary Baptist Church on whose steeple there blared away in white neon lights, visible day and night, the proletarian slogan *Where Everybody Is Somebody.* But this part of Athens Way's warm working-class welcome was, of course, lost to the Russians. The next stop was Sportsman's Bowlorama. Here the Russian visitors saw a bowling alley for the first time and watched Earlene demonstrate the game. They did not know it, but they were watching one of Los Angeles' greatest "pot bowlers" perform. Women would not bowl against Earlene, at least not for money. She had to find her competition against men, and it was at the Sportsman's Bowlorama that she could be found, sometimes all night long, putting her dollar into the pot for a winner-take-all game. The Russians did not know that they were sitting in a place where more than once Earlene had won the money she needed for rent.

High point of the tour was their visit to Reggie Brown, Earlene's 8-year-old son, who lived with his maternal grandmother. Another record was broken. No other 8-year-old in the United States had been hugged and kissed so much by so many Russian Olympic stars as Reggie Brown. Gesture and intonation overcame language barriers. Somehow Reggie managed to understand their questions about whether he wanted to be a weight-event athlete like his mother, and they in turn understood his reply that he would rather be a baseball player.

Then Earlene took her friends to the Biltmore Hotel. There they kissed each other Continental style. It had been a happy reunion. They promised to see each other that fall at Olympic Village in Tokyo at the 18th Olympiad.

Earlene Brown was an enigma. Magazines and newspapers found her good copy. It was always "jolly Earlene," "good-natured, easygoing, happy-go-lucky Earlene." In their eyes Earlene Brown did not have a care in the world.

It may come as a surprise to journalists who covered her athletic exploits to learn that nine days before she was to fly to the 1964 Tokyo Olympiad as a member of the U.S. women's Olympic team, the Los Angeles County sheriff seized her bedroom suite, her color television and her son's bicycle for nonpayment of installments totaling $68. For two months she had been away from her beauty shop, the source of her income, competing in the outdoor AAU nationals, the U.S.-USSR dual meet, and the Olympic trials. She fell two months behind in her payments.

Until Tokyo, Earlene had been in competition nine years and broke for nine years; she had never been able to train properly or to devote her

Earlene Brown throws the discus at the 1956 Olympics in Melbourne, Australia. AP/Wide World photo.

attention to improving her athletic skills because of her poor financial situation. She nearly didn't make it to the Tokyo Olympics. The AAU did not pay for an athlete's passport on overseas trips; for some strange reason, this was considered a violation of amateur rules. So Earlene had to get her own passport. The Monday training session began for the team at Rancho Cienega Playground in Los Angeles. Earlene was absent. She borrowed a

friend's car and withdrew the last $4.30 she had in her checking account.
Then she put $2.00 worth of gas in the car and drove off to a photographer
where she paid $2.00 for passport pictures. She made two telephone calls
to friends, reducing her capital to one dime, to see if she could borrow the
money for a passport. One of them said "yes," but she would have to wait
a couple of days. That Tuesday night, a writer came to her rescue, and she
paid for her passport Wednesday morning. Wednesday afternoon she was
out on the training track, two days late.

Earlene's story needs a broad canvas. There are a hundred things that
help explain her as she is, but perhaps her hands are most important. "My
mother told me," she said "that the first thing she noticed about me when
I was born were my hands." When she was about 10, she was playing the
outfield in a softball game. A ball went whizzing by. She shot up her hand
and made a one-handed Willie Mays catch. The next week she was on her
way to Oregon as a member of a softball team, and afterward, for six years,
she traveled with the team to Canada and other towns in the Northwest.
She wanted to be a shortstop, but the coach wouldn't let her. He needed
a catcher, so she contented herself with wearing a long-fingered first-
baseman's mitt and crouching behind home plate.

In 1958, Earlene established a new American record in the basketball
throw. Frances Kaszubski, of the U.S. Women's Track and Field Committee, wrote in the *Amateur Athlete*: "In the basketball throw, Earlene made
the old American record of 105 feet 9½ inches [set by Amelia Wershoven
in 1957] seem almost ridiculous by comparison with a throw of 135 feet 2
inches. This was an unbelievable 30 feet over the old record."

Earlene's record in the basketball throw came to her through a dream.
On the first day of the AAU indoor meet in Akron, Ohio, she was annoyed
by the fact that a number of smaller girls were getting more distance with
the ball than she was. She reached the conclusion that the ball was too light
for her to get distance.

> I thought about it and thought about it; I went to bed thinking about
> it; and I'll be derned if I didn't dream about it. I dreamed that I took the
> basketball and ran up with it like you do a javelin; I was holding the
> basketball just like I would a javelin. I did my cross-over step and buried
> my left foot and I whipped the ball over. It hit me in my sleep. When I
> woke up next morning, I was itching. I was the first one in the gym; I took
> the ball in my hand to see if I could handle it that way and I could. In com-
> petition, later, I threw the ball so far that it flapped up against the wall of
> the gymnasium.

Earlene's love for competitive sports made it difficult for her to have
many girls as close friends. She was too good a marble champion to play
much with dolls.

I played house and dolls when it was raining and I couldn't get out of the house. Then the little girls and I would take two chairs and put a blanket over them to make a bed. They'd get their little toys; a stove, a doll. I would make a little grass doll. I'd take a soda-pop bottle and piece of a clothesline and unravel it. Then I would put a clothespin in the bottle and tie the rope on it. I would take a matchstick and roll the rope around it and make a hairstyle.

But it didn't rain much in California, so most of the time Earlene was out playing volleyball and softball with the boys—and even football until when she was about 13, she was running toward the goal with the ball and one hard-headed little boy forgot she wasn't a boy and butted her so hard she had the wind knocked out of her. She decided then that football was not her game.

Earlene was an only child. When she was 3, her mother took Earlene and left her husband. "One thing I can say about my mother," Earlene said, "is that she might not have been rich, but everything I ventured into she tried to help me." This meant that Earlene got leotards and ballet slippers and studied ballet and exotic dancing for several years, that she finished high school and although she had no deep interest in academic studies, managed to complete all but a few hours' work for a diploma at Compton Junior College. One thing her mother did not give her was an athletic heritage. She got that from her father, who was a semipro baseball player in Texas for a number of years.

Earlene began her rise in track and field as a teenage member of the DAP, the California equivalent of the Police Athletic League in New York City. She competed in city-wide track meets in Los Angeles. In the beginning she had no idea of how to throw the discus or shot put. The big heavy teenager was a sprinter, and a good one; at least she beat the girls she ran against. She can't remember when she weighed less than 180 pounds. She could run the 100-yard dash in 12.8 seconds; she was anchor on the relay team; and she usually won the basketball throw.

Her gym teacher, Addie Valdez, introduced her to the discus, and her history teacher took her out into the schoolyard and showed her how to shot-put. But he taught her an old-fashioned method that top athletes had long since abandoned, the crossover. She was to win a national championship with this outmoded style and not change it until Perry O'Brien showed her the proper way. Soon she was winning four gold medals and a trophy for winning the baseball and basketball throws and the discus and shot put. There didn't seem to be any reason for Earlene to continue with the 100-yard dash and the relay.

Many people claim credit for discovering Earlene Brown. If they did, Earlene doesn't remember them. The fact is that Earlene had been married and given birth to her son Reggie before she considered national athletic competition. She did not join the AAU until she was 21. That was in April 1956. Three-and-a-half months later she was the new American record holder in both the shot put and the discus.

She began her rise to fame at the AAU outdoor nationals in Philadelphia in August 1956. She used sheer power to put the 4-kilogram shot 45 feet for a new American record, and she placed second in the discus, behind Pamela Kurrell, who set a new record of 140 feet, 11 inches in this event.

A week later she was competing for a place on the U.S. Olympic team. In the morning qualifying round Lois Testa, of Providence's Red Diamond AC, broke Earlene's record in the shot put with a heave of 45 feet, 6½ inches. And Earlene found herself in third place behind Paula Deubel, also from Providence.

Earlene told a reporter later, "It really hurt to lose that record." It was the first one she ever had. Right here she showed the competitive spirit that was to become her trademark. She went "off behind a barn," and while others were eating lunch, she was heaving the shot and "memorizing" the things she was doing right and the things she did wrong. Late that afternoon, Lois Testa became a former record holder when Earlene reclaimed her title with a put of 45 feet, 9½ inches.

But there was more. Pam Kurrell, who had a week-old American record, saw her title slip away when Earlene beat her record by 5 feet to set the new American record of 46 feet, 11 inches. Across America, sportswriters could not contain themselves. They saluted the new double winner in the Olympic trials; Earlene's star was rising. But there was one dissenter: her young husband. In a marital disagreement, Earlene and her husband separated. Eight years later, Earlene recognized the heavy burden her athletic victories placed on her husband. All of a sudden he found that he was "Earlene Brown's husband." She had written a role for herself in a play in which he had no part. At first he tried to join the act by serving as her coach, but he had never been a coach or track athlete, and he and Earlene soon realized that his coaching was not what she needed.

As Earlene said, "I called myself behaving like a proper wife. To start off with, I asked him if I could go. That was a mistake, because I gave him the authority to tell me whether or not I could go. He ordered me not to go."

It did not seem to Earlene that asking a young husband to take over the care of a 5-month-old son while the mother was traipsing off to the Olympics in Melbourne 10,000 miles away, was wrong. And while the newspapers were describing the fun Earlene, Pam Kurrell, and Willye B. White were having in the Olympic Village teaching the Russians and Nigerians how to do the rock 'n' roll, Earlene was griving over the unhappiness of a broken marriage.

Earlene's outward behavior always belied her inner feelings. It simply wasn't possible for her Olympic field coach to imagine that this 265-pound, 5-feet-9-inch Amazon was undergoing the anxiety of a very feminine wife and mother. "Even though I rebelled against him," Earlene said, "I still had this unhappiness in me."

These inner tensions were at war with the excitement of Earlene's first Olympiad. A thousand doves, thousands of athletes speaking almost every language in the world, a hundred thousand spectators—all made for a mighty motivation. Earlene did not win, but she did improve her American record.

Melbourne opened a new world for Earlene. Her athletic powers had taken her halfway around the earth. Everywhere she had gone in the Olympic Village she had been popular. Australian, Russian, and Nigerian athletes sought her out. There was something warm and easygoing about the big powerful brown girl in white horn-rimmed glasses who was as light on her feet as a ballerina.

From the beginning, Earlene made long-lasting friendships with her fellow American athletes. There was Pam Kurrell, whom she met in Washington, D.C., and was her roommate in Melbourne, and Sharon Shepard. In 1957 there was Olga Connolly, who as Olga Fikotovaa had won the discus at Melbourne while representing Czechoslovakia. Olga, now an American citizen, had fallen in love with the American hammer thrower Harold Connolly and married him. At the AAU outdoor nationals held in Cleveland, Ohio, suburb of Shaker Heights, Connolly won the discus throw. Earlene was second, but won the shot put championship for a second year. For the next four years women's weight events in America were dominated by Earlene, Pamela, Olga, and Sharon.

Early in July 1958 the outdoor nationals of the AAU were held in Monmouth, New Jersey. Winners at the meet were to compose the U.S. team scheduled to compete in Europe that August. Earlene had prepared for this meet. She had gotten her weight down and was in peak condition. The prospect of a European trip gave her a keen edge.

Earlene started off with a shot put heave of 47 feet, 5½ inches, which broke her old American record and won first place. She told reporters: "I don't want it to sound like bragging, but honestly, I thought I could do better. I have been throwing the shot put 49 and ¼ feet regularly. The underfooting here was kind of soft—probably too soft for a heavyweight like me." Then she won a gold medal in the discus with a throw of 152 feet, 5½ inches. On her trip to Europe she had won two gold medals and set one new record.

The foreign meets began in Russia, and Earlene was a standout favorite with the crowds. On Moscow streets she was surrounded by throngs of autograph seekers. The Associated Press reported: "Mrs. Earlene

Brown is the toast of Moscow, just as she was the most widely known of the United States athletes in the Olympic Village in Melbourne in 1956."

Earlene had not been bragging when she told reporters she was regularly throwing the shot nearly 50 feet in practice. Training in Moscow, she surprised herself and her coach by throwing it over 50 feet. This was a first for any American athlete. She had still to test her strength against the Russians. She did, and she beat the best of them. This is what the record looked like:

> First: Earlene Brown, United States, 54 feet, 3½ inches
> Second: Galina Zybina, USSR, 52 feet, 11½ inches
> Third: Tamara Press, USSR, 52 feet, 3½ inces
> Fourth: Sharon Shepard, United States, 44 feet, 9½ inches

Earlene had beaten the best in Russia, and her nearest American competitor was nearly 10 feet behind. In the discus, the Russian athlete Nina Ponomkareva was first with a throw of 171 feet, but Earlene was second, throwing the discus more than 162 feet.

Then came Warsaw. For Earlene it meant two gold medals for a first place in the shot put and the discus. It also meant a round of fun. Earlene remembers the gaiety of Warsaw nightclubs. At night, when practice was over, athletes from several countries would go together in some café where there was entertainment and dancing. When they left, there would be money from all the countries spread on the table to pay the bill, a babel of currencies.

And when Earlene went sightseeing alone, she would invariably get lost. She went for a walk in Budapest and soon discovered she could not find the way back to her hotel. Crowds gathered around her, smiled, and spoke to her in Hungarian. Earlene smiled back but still didn't know which way to turn. Finally she took the hand of a smiling man, put it in hers, and pushed him in the direction she thought she needed to go. He led her back to her hotel.

Athens was bright and sunny. The dual meet with Greece was held in the Panathenian Stadium, the same one that had been used in 1896 for the first modern Olympic Games. At that time Robert Garrett, an American, had won the discus with a throw of a little over 95 feet. But the stadium was not prepared for another American discus thrower who would come along 62 years later. When Earlene picked up the discus and began to build up power by rapidly swirling her body around, the audience had no way of judging her strength. She hurled the discus 155 feet, 8¾ inches, more than 15 feet beyond the mark of teammate Pam Kurrell and 60 feet beyond the best mark of the male American who first threw the discus there. Indeed, Earlene threw the discus clear out of the stadium and up into the stands. It hit two people. When she learned this, Earlene ran over to the spectator seats with an interpreter. A woman she had hit was rubbing her ankle and talking rapidly. Earlene was concerned. She asked: "Did you tell her I am sorry?" "Yes." said the interpreter. "What did she say?" "She said, 'That's alright; it doesn't hurt much; but could I have your autograph.'" Earlene laughed and put her arms around the Greek woman while the crowd roared with laughter.

In Athens she won first place in the shot put over her teammate Sharon Shepard. She had won the national championships in the discus and shot put in the United States and had beaten the best weight-eventers in Europe, bringing back seven gold medals and one silver medal. And she was the only American woman who had ever shot-put over 50 feet. In two short years Earlene Dennis Brown had risen to the top ranks of American athletes, taking her place in company with Mildred "Babe" Didrikson.

In 1959 Earlene was still the toast of AAU officials. They had never seen anyone like her. They took it for granted that like most maturing athletes, she would improve with time. No one paid any attention to her training program.

The hard necessity of earning a livelihood for herself and her son was consuming most of Earlene's time. Her days were spent attending Henrietta's Beauty College learning to be a beautician. She worked long hours in a stuffy cubicle washing, drying, pressing, and curling women's hair. The long hours of standing on her feet and the fumes of hair oils made Earlene too tired to undertake the kind of rigorous training necessary to an athlete.

But this was not the only reason she could not train. Earlene has always been frank about her weaknesses. "Coaches were always asking me to train the way they wanted me to train. They were always telling me to run two laps around the track and do setting-up exercises. I would run around the track for one lap just to please the coach, but if he wanted two, he would have to run the second one himself." Most of the time she had no athletic-club affiliation, no team loyalty to spur her on to group achievement. She had no way to train seriously before competition.

Despite the unevenness of her training programs, Earlene still gave a good account of herself in 1959. She won the AAU outdoor national championships in the shot put and discus and bettered her own 1958 record in the discus with a new throw of 153 feet, 8 inches. She represented the United States at Chicago that year in the Pan-American Games where she set new meet records in both the shot put and the discus.

The dual meet between the USSR and the United States was held in Philadelphia. The previous year Earlene had won a gold medal in the shot put. This year she took second place. Tamara Press, who put a little better

than 52 feet in 1958, now heaved the shot more than 55½ feet to beat the
world record, while Earlene put the shot 3 feet less than she had the
previous year. Still, her distance was a respectable 51 feet, 6½ inches. In
the discus she finished third, with Nina Ponomkareva and Yevgeniya
Kuznetsova ahead of her. On the surface it was a successful year for
Earlene, but only if you were willing to overlook the great athletic potential
in her which had failed to materialize.

Sitting in the Biltmore Hotel one Sunday during the summer of 1964,
somebody said to Earlene, "Let's talk about the race problem." And
Earlene said, "Me living here in Los Angeles, I never ran into it in my life."
Then she said with a quick smile, "I take that lie back," as she started to
tell the story of a motor trip through Texas with two white athletes:

> I will never forget the first time I ever did run into the race problem. I
> was going to the outdoor nationals in Corpus Christi. Pam [Kurrell],
> Sharon [Shepard], and I decided we did not want to fly over and that we
> would rent a car and drive over. Pam came down from San Francisco and
> met Sharon and me there.
>
> Well, on the road we drove and drove, and we got hungry and stopped
> at a restaurant. We went in, sat down, and grabbed a menu, and a lady
> came over and said, "I am sorry, we can't serve you." And it hit me. I said,
> "Oh my goodness, this is Texas."
>
> Sharon and Pam got mad, and I said, "No use to get mad. There's a
> whole state of it." I said, "You order me a sandwich or something, and
> I'll go back to the car and wait." They wouldn't hear that. They wanted
> to prove their friendship to me. They wouldn't eat in the place if I couldn't
> eat with them. So we went down the street, and we finally found a little
> place where they would let the three of us eat together back in the kitchen.
> So we went back into the kitchen where the food was prepared, and there
> were horseflies all over the food. The place was filthy. I said, "Shoot, Pam,
> if the food is this dirty, I don't want to eat here, period." We were about
> fifty miles from Corpus Christi, and I said, "I can hold out if you can."
> And Pam said, "I can," and Sharon said, "Let's go." Heck, I couldn't see
> why they were so prejudiced when they were serving garbage like that.

But Jim Crow did not mar Earlene's performance. At Corpus Christi
she won the international championships in the discus and shot put. Then
she went to the Olympic trial meet in Abilene and threw the discus farther
than any other American woman in history ever had. She set a record of
176 feet, 10½ inches. Her shot put distance of 50 feet, 10 inches made her
a double winner with Wilma Rudolph at the trials and set a new Olympic
trials record, breaking her own 1956 record.

Earlene took part in a limbering-up meet, the U.S.A. Relay Championships, in Buffalo, New York, before the Olympic Games in Rome. She won
the discus throw with an effort of over 171 feet, but a curious part of her
record is the gold medal she won in that meet for throwing the javelin—all

of 118 feet. A good performance with the javelin is closer to 200 feet. There were many American women who could throw the javelin more than 150 feet. To Earlene, the javelin was like throwing a toothpick. She couldn't get her hands on it; she couldn't get her force behind it. It was like the basketball throw all over, but this time she had no saving dream.

Eleven black girls and five white girls made up the U.S. women's Olympic team at Rome. Earlene was mother of them all. She organized the dancing at the Olympic Village and the card playing. The boxers Eddie Machen and Cassius Clay [now Mohammed Ali] were her buddies. She was the most popular of the American athletes, at least until Wilma Rudolph won three gold medals. Everybody came to her to get her signature in a book or on an Olympic souvenir. Earlene never turned them down. "Signing autographs is a key to your popularity, because a lot of them [athletes] don't want to be bothered by little people. I enjoy it. I always did. Lots of times Wilma and I would get caught signing autographs. Once you stopped to sign one, you could look to get tied up, and you just kept signing until you signed yourself right into the gate at Olympic Village."

A special friendship existed between Wilma and Earlene that expressed itself in a number of ways. For example, one newspaper reported this experience: "Wilma is just a lovely person, too. After winning the first of her three gold medals in the 100-yard dash, she politely freed herself from press, photographers and well wishers and sped the length of the Olympic stadium to give a grateful embrace to the mother of the U.S. Women's team, Mrs. Earlene Brown." Earlene and Barbara Jones were there waiting for her with a towel and comb ready to enforce the Tennessee State rule that female athletes be allowed to "pretty up" before the cameras start clicking.

After Wilma's victories in the 100 meters and 200 meters, Earlene took third place in the shot put. She had qualified for the finals without even taking off her sweat suit. She was sixth in the discus. She might have done better, but she had become involved in an argument with some of the administrators of the American team. This is Earlene's side of the controversy:

> I was depressed at Rome. We had a lot of politics going on that year—
> what I call politics. When you say Russian and the United States have to
> go to a tea and that it's compulsory to go—to me this is politics. I felt that
> we were there in Rome, Italy, and the Italians were our hosts and they told
> us the United States team must go to a tea for the Russians. I wouldn't
> go. So I caused quite a lot of trouble that year because I wouldn't go. I
> was ready to come home without competing. All they had to do was give
> me my ticket.
>
> I think a lot of times they go out of their way to try to be friends when

all they have to do is be themselves. You don't have to promote different things like this. You shouldn't cater to people to be their friends. You don't have to buy friendship. You be yourself and be a good person and you automatically have a friend.

But the disagreement over the Russian tea party blew over. If Earlene did not take tea with the Russians, she was singing and dancing with the Russian athletes all over the Olympic Village, and it is doubtful that she was even missed at the tea. But the glib sportswriters, who were busy depicting Earlene as a smiling child of nature, failed to understand the depths of the revolution inside her. Earlene was stubborn, with a mind of her own.

Less than three weeks after the Rome Olympics, Earlene set a new American record in the shot put of 54 feet, 9 inches, just 2 feet less than the winning put of Tamara Press, who won the event's gold medal at Rome. This was at Frankfort, Germany, in a dual meet with the West Germans. No one can say what Earlene might have done in Rome if "politics" had not been an issue, but what is clear is the fact that the American star did not give her best performance at Rome.

After Frankfort, there were other meets. Earlene won the shot put and discus in the British Commonwealth Games in London. She returned to the Panathenian Stadium in bright and sunny Athens. This time she threw the discus over 171 feet. She didn't hit a spectator this time, but she still had to sign hundreds of autographs. And in Greece Earlene received the welcome befitting an Olympic champion. She climbed the Acropolis in Athens and swam in the strong surf of the Aegean Sea. But she was careful not to go in over her head. Swimming was Earlene's Achilles' heel. She has never trusted herself in water over her head.

Cynthia Wyatt, of the University of Hawaii, was national indoor champion in the shot put in 1961. Her winning throw went just 39 feet, 11 inches, almost 15 feet less than Earlene's effort at Frankfort. The University of Hawaii paid the expenses for Cynthia to make the trip to the AAU indoor meet in Columbus, Ohio. Earlene simply could not afford to compete. She did, however, manage to defend her championships in the shot put and the discus at the outdoor nationals. She placed first in each event. She had trained for only a week and had fallen far below her record performances in these events. It was a sorry performance but still better than any of her competitors'. She was chosen to represent the United States on its tour of Europe.

But Earlene could not go. She had just bought a beauty shop for $10,000 with a down payment of $1,000. She had to fix up the shop, get operators to work for her, and attract some customers. Nearly $50 a month went for interest on her mortgage. The fact that Earlene was one of the greatest women athletes of all times wasn't worth a wooden nickel to her business. Most of her customers neither knew nor cared. So she passed up what was dearest to her heart, another trip to Moscow, Warsaw, and Germany representing the United States. Staying home solved no problems. In her beauty shop she was forced to work long hours just to keep her head above water financially.

Since she was endowed with a fine physical build, some of Earlene's friends thought she ought to apply for a position as a Los Angeles policewoman. Here was a job with a decent salary and a pension. Earlene disagreed. "Shoot, I couldn't be a policewoman. I'm too softhearted. Give me a sad story, and I'd let the crook go. Besides, I've got too many friends—some crooked and some not crooked, and I'd have to look the other way. I just couldn't be a policewoman."

If ever there was a clear case of how American concepts of amateurism stifles the development of American athletes, that case would be Earlene Brown. While Russian women had undergone almost constant training in their athletic specialties, with job security, housing, and other creature comforts fully provided by the state, a great natural athlete like Earlene had to fend for herself. A great American star who had brought great prestige to the United States at the height of the cold war by beating Russia's finest athlete in Moscow in 1962 was hard-put even to make the U.S. team.

The AAU outdoor nationals in 1962 were held in Los Angeles, and Earlene shuttled between her beauty shop and the stadium to compete. In a morning qualifying round for the shot put Earlene found herself barely qualifying, finishing in fifth place. She was close to defeat. Again she used her lunch hour for some last-minute training. The finals followed. Her first puts in the finals still left her out of contention. Then, on her final throw, in one mighty effort, she came from behind and put the shot 48 feet, 10½ inches. Once again she had won the national championship. But she was not so lucky in the discus. Here Olga Connolly took first, and Earlene had to settle for second. In the meet between the United States and Russia in Palo Alto, beaten in Moscow in 1958, Tamara Press put the shot just over 57 feet, and Earlene placed third with a put under 50 feet.

Earlene's problems escalated in 1963. Her beauty shop was an unending tangle of headaches, and she simply did not have the time to train. She lost her outdoor AAU national title in the shot put to Sharon Shepard, who in previous years had been anywhere between 5 and 10 feet behind Earlene's mark. Earlene couldn't even take second place in the discus or the shot put. She was barely beaten by Cynthia Wyatt of the University of Ohio. The consequence was that she was denied the opportunity to represent the United States in the Pan-American Games in Sao Paulo, Brazil, and in the European meets in Russia, Poland, Germany, England, and Greece. It was a bitter defeat.

Some shook their heads, as if to say "This is the end of Earlene Brown and international competition." The fact was, however, that no new champion had posted a new and better mark in the discus or shot put. The AAU champions in 1962 had given only mediocre performances. It was not just the low point of Earlene's career; it was a sad moment for the U.S. competition, for with a very ordinary performance, Nancy McCredie of Canada was able to take the gold medals in the shot put and discus in the Pan-American Games.

"A hundred times I've said I'd quit," said Earlene, "but each time I'd get the old urge to travel, and I'd be at it again." In 1964 Earlene was "at it again." She began her comeback at the outdoor nationals in Hanford, California. A put of 46 feet, 11 inches was enough for first place in the shot put, and a heave of 156 feet, 8 inches brought her into second place in the discus behind Olga Connolly. Then came the dual meet between the Soviet Union and the United States. She placed third in the shot put. Tamara Press and Galina Zybina were first and second. She placed fourth in the discus behind two Russians and Olga.

Her main test came at the Olympic trials held in August at Randall's Island in New York City. She was her old self. She swept away the competition, including Sharon Shepard and Cynthia Wyatt, just as she had between 1956 and 1962. She placed second to Olga Connolly in the discus, but her mark did not meet qualifying standards for Olympic competition. After her debacle of 1963, Earlene had staged a comeback. She had won a place for the third consecutive time on the U.S. women's Olympic team. She was one of three women, along with Mae Faggs and Willye B. White, who had done so.

In Los Angeles, where the Olympic team gathered for preliminary training, Earlene had just three days of training, barely enough time to limber up. Earlene and the coach, Jack Griffin, knew she was far behind in her training schedule, so she had to work hard before the team left for Tokyo. Once in Japan, she practiced hard at the University of Tokyo, but there were less than two weeks to train before the competition began. In the qualifying round she ranked seventh with a put of 50 feet, 7 inches— once again over the magic 50-foot mark. Between July and October three meets and a few weeks of training had improved her performance by almost four feet. It is painful to reflect on what her performance might have been with anything like the three months of intensive training each Russian athlete had before the Tokyo Olympics.

In the finals she did not equal her qualifying mark; she fell back to twelfth place with a put of 48 feet, 6 inches. She had won no medals, but in qualifying for the finals, she had established the unique record of being the only athlete in the world ever to reach the finals in the shot put in three consecutive Olympics.

While she was in Japan, Earlene had secret worries. How was she going to pick up the pieces of her wrecked finances when she returned to Los Angeles? How would she find a place to live? What would she use for money? But looking at her, you would never know about her troubles. She was too busy making sunshine for everyone else, especially the youngsters on the team. She would sit on a bed with Debbie Thompson, helping her with her high school mathematics so that the young athlete might keep up with her studies back in Frederick, Maryland. She might have lost all of her customers in her Los Angeles beauty shop, but she had nearly all the girls on the team as her customers, and with the rain and drizzle in Tokyo added to running and jumping, Earlene was kept busy. Most of the time she was a settling force for the whole team. She had been "Mother" in Rome; she was "Mother" in Tokyo too.

Just as she had in every foreign city she had visited, Earlene lost no time in making Tokyo her own. She learned the city inside out. She went shopping on the Ginza for wigs to sell in her Los Angeles beauty shop. She rode in Tokyo's suicidal taxis and even found a bowling alley. It wasn't long before Earlene introduced an unscheduled "Olympic Event" to Japan, pot bowling. She didn't get a gold medal, but she did win $50 in Japanese yen.

In Tokyo it was old-home week for Earlene. The Russians, the Germans, the Australians, the Nigerians—all would greet her, embrace her, and say in any language they could speak how glad they were that she was competing in another Olympic game. One day, more than half the Italian Olympic team, who remembered her from Rome, came to get her so that their official photographer could take their picture with her. Her popularity glowed despite her poor performance. Athletes of many nations recognized her as one of the great American athletes of all times. The United States never had a better or wiser ambassador of goodwill.

Earlene did not return from Japan without a medal. Japan and the United States competed in the British Commonwealth Games in Osaka. There Earlene won a gold medal in the shot put and a silver medal in the discus, contributing 15 points to the team's score.

Sports was a way of life for Earlene, a road that led if only temporarily from the ghetto to the rest of the world, a world she may never have seen had it not been for her athletic ability. Reflecting on her athletic career, she said:

> Sports is the greatest thing for any individual to have. Without sports I would have been nothing. I don't see where life would have had any meaning. I must be on this earth for a reason because God has blessed me. He's given me the opportunity to see the world, something even most rich folks are not going to see.

Judi Brown

Judi Brown won a silver medal on the 400 meter hurdles at the 1984 Los Angeles Olympiad with a time of 55.20 seconds.

Terrezene Brown

Terrezene Brown was a high jumper on the 1964 U.S. Olympic team.

Vivian D. Brown

Vivian D. Brown, a 100- and 200-meter sprinter, competed in the 1960 Olympics in Rome. A member of the Tennessee State University Tigerbelle team, she was from Chicago.

Rosalyn Bryant

Rosalyn Bryant competed on the U.S.A.'s team to the 1976 Montreal Olympics and won a silver medal for the relay team's second-place finish in the 1600-meter relay. She also placed fifth in the 400-meter run.

Robin Campbell

Robin Campbell ran in the 800 meters at the 1984 Olympics in Los Angeles, California.

Chandra Cheeseborough

Chandra Cheeseborough won a gold medal at the 1984 Olympics in Los Angeles, California, as a member of the U.S. 400-meter relay team.

**Vivian Brown (right) beats Maria Itklina, the Soviet Union's best woman
sprinter in the 200-meter dash at the 1962 dual U.S.A.-USSR track meet at
Stanford, California. AP/Wide World photo.**

She won a silver medal that year for a second-place finish in the 400-meter
run. She won a second gold medal in Los Angeles as a member of the
U.S.A.'s record-setting 4×400 (1600 meters) relay team.

Alice Coachman

There were no Olympic Games in 1940 and 1944 because of World
War II. With international competition almost wholly eliminated except
for dual meets with Canada, a great deal of the impetus behind women's
track and field was lost. Interest in the sports dwindled. One oasis in this
athletic wasteland was Tuskegee Institute, and this was due largely to the
pioneer effort of Major Cleveland Abbott, who developed the Tuskegee
Relays. Beginning in 1936, the Tuskegee Relays was the proving ground for
a score of young black girls from high schools in Alabama, Georgia, and

other southern states. Many of the better athletes at the relays were re-
cruited for a summer program of track and field at the institute, and some
of these were offered work scholarships to attend Tuskegee Institute.

This concentration of good athletes paid off. Tuskegee began winning
national track-and-field meets of the AAU in 1937; by 1946, it had won 10
outdoor national meets. Indeed, from 1937 through 1956, except for 1952,
there was at least one Tuskegee girl among the AAU outdoor national
champions. For nearly 20 years Tuskegee dominated women's track and
field in the United States.

Among the stars on the Tuskegee track team were many who might
have made the U.S. Olympic team if there had been Olympiads in 1940 and
1944. Certainly one of these was Lula Hymes from Booker T. Washington
High School in Atlanta, Georgia. She was team captain from 1937 to 1939
and ran anchor on Tuskegee's winning 400-meter relay team three years
in a row. She was AAU national champion in the long jump in 1937 and
1938, and in the 100 meters in 1939. She equaled the world record in the
100 meters in 1939. Her one chance to make the Olympic team came in
1936 when she was a freshman at Tuskegee, but she failed. She said: "It
was my first year in strong competition and I guess I just plain froze up.
Just plain frightened. When the time came to go, I was left at my starting
blocks."

Unquestionably the most outstanding of Tuskegee's long list of stars
was Alice Coachman (Davis) of Albany, Georgia. With the exception of
Stella Walsh, she has won more national championships than any other
American woman—26. Coachman was the national outdoor high jump
champion for 10 straight years, 1939 through 1948, and outdoor 50 meters
champion for five years, 1943 through 1947.

In 1946 Coachman was a triple winner of the 50 meters, the 100
meters, and the high jump, contributing 30 of the 95 points earned by the
Tuskegee team to win the national outdoor meet. In 1946 she was the only
black woman chosen to be a member of the U.S. team which competed
against Canada. In the dual U.S.A.-Canada meet she won the 100 meters,
the high jump, and ran anchor on the 400-meter relay team. A caption
under a picture of the U.S. team in one newspaper read:

> Miss Alice Coachman, on the left, is the only Negro member of the
> United States National A.A.U. Team which competed in Canada. Miss
> Coachman was under careful scrutiny before being selected to go on the
> trip. The committee found her to be quiet, ladylike, reserved and most
> desirable. In addition to athletic prowess, she's a fine person to know on
> and off the track.

When at last the Olympic Games were scheduled again, to take place
in London's Wembley Stadium, it was Alice who led a strong contingent

Alice Coachman sets an Olympic record of 5 feet, 6½ inches at London's Wembley Stadium during the 1948 Olympics. She was the first black woman to win an Olympic gold medal and the only American female gold medal winner at the London Games. Courtesy United States Olympic Committee.

of Tuskegee girls to the Olympic trials in Providence, Rhode Island. There were mishaps on the Tuskegee squad. Two of the best runners failed to qualify. One was Juanita Watson, a powerful little runner from Bessemer, Alabama. Her teammates had nicknamed her Mighty Mouse. In 1945 she had beaten Walsh to become outdoor 100 meters champion, and she had won the indoor national championship in the 50 meters. She had been a member of Tuskegee's winning outdoor and indoor relay teams for two years and was national champion in the baseball throw. The other athlete was Tuskegee's best hurdler, Lillie Purifoy, three times national outdoor champion in the 50-meter hurdles. In the trial she struck the fourth hurdle while leading her competitors, had a nasty fall, and could not finish.

When the trials were over, the *St. Louis Post-Dispatch* wrote: "Eleven speedy and muscular women were picked today for the United States Women's Track and Field Team." Nine of the 11 were black, and 4 of these came from Tuskegee Institute. Tennessee State, which had begun a program of women's track in 1947, had two athletes qualify: Audrey Patterson, who won the 200-meter run, and Emma Reed, who won the long jump. Originally a Redwood, Mississippi, farm girl, Reed had been entered in the high jump and placed third, but she was so afraid that she might not make the team that she entered the long jump and won it. She had never competed in the event. Washington Park Playground, of Chicago, also qualified two athletes: Bernice Robinson, who had won the outdoor national championship in the 80-meter hurdles and Lillian Young. New York's PAL qualified the soon-to-be famous Mae Faggs. The four Tuskegee athletes were Mabel Walker, who won the 100 meters; Nell Jackson, who ran second behind Tennessee's Audrey Patterson in the 200 meters; Theresa Manuel, who qualified in both the hurdles and the javelin; and Alice Coachman.

Alice won the high jump in near darkness. Officials lit matches so the contestants could see, and Alice put a borrowed white handkerchief on the bar to show her where she had to jump. She set a new Olympic trials record that was not broken until the 1960 trials.

Only two white American girls made the team: Frances Kaszubski of the Polish Olympic Women's Athletic Club of Cleveland, the club made famous by Stella Walsh's membership, and Dorothy Dodson of the Chicago Hurricanes. Both were field-eventers. The year 1948 was the beginning of a period when black athletes played a dominant role on U.S. women's Olympic teams. Not since then have black women been less than a majority of any American women's Olympic track-and-field team.

The *St. Louis Post-Dispatch*'s snide comment about "muscular women" was a reflection of the then-current image of American women athletes. Babe Didrikson and Helen Stephens had been short-haired, lanky, and "mannish-looking." The idea of women running, jumping, and throwing contradicted the popular American concept of women as dainty, cuddly, and feminine. The truth is that few if any of the members of the 1948 team were muscular; most were extremely young and feminine.

They were quite human too. Although she was the veteran of the team, Alice Coachman cried when she found herself alone in a stateroom aboard the SS *America*. Her cabinmate then became 14-year-old Mae Faggs, whom the team coach, Catherine Myers, placed with Alice to keep her from getting homesick. It worked just the other way. The bouncy 14-year-old, with a small jar of hard candy always with her, kept Alice's spirits high.

For most of the girls on the team, it was a first trip abroad. Fruits, nuts, ice cream, cookies, and course after course of rich food on the ship's menu were heavy temptations to girls who were young and poor and trying to stay in shape for the most important athletic event of their lives. Team member Nell Jackson observed many years later: "Sometimes I think we ate ourselves out of some of the races on the boat." There were other calamities. During the first day at sea the Tuskegee girls discovered that Coach Abbott had forgotten to pack a supply of Dr. George Washington Carver's peanut oil, a famous product they used in rubdowns. So Coach Harry Hainsworth cabled Tuskegee to have the institute rush a supply to London. It came on the next boat.

There was also fun on the *America*. Everyone was relaxed and confident. Everyone looked forward to this first Olympic contest in 12 years. On July 19, at the ship's concert, the women's Olympic track-and-field team entertained the other passengers. Alice Coachman danced to the "St. Louis Blues," Bernice Robinson, the hurdler sang "Without a Song," and Henry F. Dreir, the hammer thrower, pleased the crowd with his rendition of "The Girl That I Marry." It was a happy group of American athletes.

It was not long, however, before gloom settled over the American team. "I was disgusted," said Alice Coachman, "because we thought we had some of the fastest girls, and they kept getting eliminated." The cause of much of the discomfiture was a 30-year-old Dutch woman, the mother of two children, Fanny Blankers-Koen of Amsterdam. That year she was unbeatable. She won the 100 meters, the 200 meters, and the 80-meter hurdles, and ran anchor on the winning 400-meter relay team—four gold medals. Only one American girl, Audrey Patterson of Tennessee State, came close to her; she ran third in the 200 meters. Allison Danzig of the *New York Times* wrote: "Audrey Williamson [of Great Britain] just got home ahead of Audrey Patterson of Tennessee State College, who surprised in taking third place for the United States, which had little chance to cheer in women's track and field."

It was a grudging comment by an observer who had watched all week long as American sprinters were eliminated in the trial heats. It was no better in the field events. An Austrian girl had won the javelin throw; a Hungarian girl was first in the broad jump; and Michelline Ostermeyer of France had taken two gold medals, in the shot put and the discus. The same Mrs. Ostermeyer was entered in the high jump and had qualified for the finals. In all these field events the American women had not scored a single point. "Little chance to cheer," indeed.

The women's high jump was the last event on the last day of the Olympic Games. Alice spent her off-track time high up on top of a London double-decker bus sightseeing in towns like Putney, Hammersmith, and other suburbs. Now it was her turn to compete. It was the last chance for the American women's team to win a gold medal. It was the last chance too for Great Britain to win a gold medal. The *New York Times* story said:

> All week the British had been swarming to Wembley in amazing numbers in torrid heat, mist and rain. Day after day they had turned out with the hope of seeing one of their heroes gain a victory that would permit them to hear "God Save the King" instead of national anthems of the United States and Sweden over and over again. Day after day they had seen their men defeated, and their fine women athletes forced to take second place to the amazing Mrs. Fanny Blankers-Koen of the Netherlands.

The competition dragged on. Alice, wearing the foot-high numerals 755 on her back, continued to go over the bar. Finally, the bar reached 5 feet 3 inches, and the field was narrowed to three jumpers: Michelline Ostermeyer of France, already a winner of two gold medals; Mrs. Dorothy Tyler of Great Britain, who had competed in the Berlin Olympic Games; and Alice Coachman. The British crowd was waiting for a triumph on this last day. It was late afternoon, but there were still more than 50,000 spectators in the stands. It had been a long, grueling competition. Finally, Ostermeyer was eliminated, but both Coachman and Tyler cleared the bar at 5 feet 6½ inches. Alice was declared winner because she had had fewer misses in preceding jumps. "I didn't know I had won until my name went up on the board," she said. She had won the first gold medal for the American women's team; she had prevented the British fans from hearing the bands play "God Save the King"; she had brought fame to Georgia, her native state.

She was greeted by Americans all over London and exchanged autographs with movie actor Fredric March and Virginia-born Lady Nancy Astor, who gave a tea for the American girls. After the London Olympic Games, Alice competed in a dual meet with France in Paris. There, with no Fanny Blankers-Koen to interfere, she won the 100 meters and the high jump, and ran anchor on the winning relay team.

When she returned to the United States, she went to the White House and was personally congratulated by President Harry S Truman. Then she went home to Georgia.

Her widowed mother, Mrs. Evelyn Coachman, was waiting. It had been hard bringing Alice and her brothers up after the death of her husband. She lived in constant fear that Alice would "hurt herself." She told one reporter: "Many times I had to go to loan companies to get Alice the things she needed; but somehow we've always managed." Now, with an Olympic gold medal in the family, the sacrifices had been justified.

An Alice Coachman Day was planned for Albany, her hometown. There was a motorcade from Atlanta, and thousands lined the road to cheer as the motorcade wound its way through the small towns of Montezuma and Americus on the way to Albany's Municipal Auditorium. Huge floats met her at the city limits. *Time* and *Life* magazines and Movietone News covered the event. Marion E. Jackson of the *Atlanta Daily World* wrote with southern eloquence in his column "Sports of the World":

> Let me write now that until the parade terminated at the auditorium, Georgia had seen democracy in action. It was not a homecoming for a Negro Olympic star, but a champion of champions. As I watched the faces of thousands of Georgians from all over the state it was interesting to note, that all of their prejudices, preferences, passions and hates were momentarily swept from their countenances as if a heavy rainstorm had drenched a mountainous street. They came to applaud, cheer and praise an agile, slim and speedy star whose flying feet had brought her acclaim not only from her home state, but from the forums of the world. And then my dream was shattered. Reality returned and I knew that Georgia would not make Alice's welcome a wholehearted one. Mayor James W. "Taxi" Smith droned on about Georgia's other Olympic champion [Forrest "Spec" Towns who had won the 110-meter hurdles twelve years earlier, in the 1936 Olympics]. He never shook her hand nor did he look at her. Alice never got a chance to speak.

The auditorium was segregated. Even on the platform, Alice and black dignitaries were separated from the mayor and other white citizens by a black baby-grand piano. Furtively, behind the platform, two anonymous white women handed Alice a dozen American Beauty roses with no card.

But it didn't matter. Her sorority, Delta Sigma Theta, made up for the chill of official Albany with a banquet whose menu commemorated her triumph and her fondest memories.

Olympic Menu
Soup à la Coachman
High Jump Chicken
Grand Rapid Peas Providence Potatoes Delight
U.S. America Tossed Salad
Lady Astor Tea Wembley Stadium Rolls
"Jolly Ole" Ice Cream
with
Hot Champion Fudge
and
Albany Nuts and Candy

What mattered most for Alice Coachman was that her 1948 high jump won the only gold medal for America. As the first black woman athlete to win one in Olympic competition, she had started the first leg of a long relay of supremacy for black women in the Olympics.

Shirley Crowder

Few track-and-field events hold more peril for the contestants than the hurdles. Lillie Purifoy of Tuskegee, one of the best hurdlers of her day, failed to make the 1948 Olympic team because she kicked over the fourth hurdle in her trial meet. Tidye Pickett made the team and went to Berlin in 1936, but she too hit a hurdle in her trial heat and limped home in third place. One of the unluckiest of the hurdlers was Shirley Crowder of Tennessee State.

Shirley was a tall and rangy farm girl from Temple, Georgia, where she had ample opportunity to run and jump with her six sisters and four brothers. When her family moved to Atlanta, she entered Booker T. Washington High School where she became a star basketball player. Because she was a natural athlete, the transition from basketball to track was easy for her. In 1955 and 1956 she spent a month in Coach Cleve Abbott's track clinic in Tuskegee, and at the end of the 1956 program she competed in the AAU outdoor national meet in Philadelphia. She won the 50-yard hurdles in the girls' division, but in the women's division she tripped over a hurdle and had a nasty fall. The next week, before the Olympic trials in Washington, was spent nursing her bruises and getting ready for the great test. In the trials she qualified for the finals. As she took her mark for the final race, an announcement was made over the loudspeaker asking that an ambulance be brought onto the field. Her fall the previous week was uppermost in her mind. "I was sure he was ordering that ambulance for me; it worried me, but I began the race and I was leading up to the seventh hurdle. Then I did it again; I tripped over the hurdle, and there went my chance to make the Olympic team."

Shirley entered Tennessee State on a track scholarship. In 1957 she won the 80-meter hurdle championship in the AAU outdoor meet easily, and in 1958 an opportunity to compete for membership on the American team bound for Russia came up. This time she did not get a chance to trip over the hurdle. Over anxious, she disqualified herself with two false starts before the race was run. She had missed the boat again.

It almost seemed that Shirley could win only when no overseas travel was involved in the victory, for in 1959, when the Russian team came to

Philadelphia, she again won the AAU championship and was on the U.S. team which met the Russians. She placed fourth in her event, won by Galina Bystrova of Russia.

Shirley won her first opportunity to represent the United States overseas in 1960 when she won a place on the team chosen for the Rome Olympiad. She almost lost that chance. She lost her national championship at Corpus Christi, Texas, to teammate Jo Ann Terry, but she came back strong a week later at the Olympic trials in Abilene to beat Jo Ann. Both of them made the team. Shirley, at last, had beaten her jinx. The competition in Rome was too hard for both girls. They were eliminated in their trial heats. For Shirley it was the end of competition. Jo Ann continued to compete for two more years.

There was something bittersweet for the black athlete in the experience of marching behind the American flag in Rome. A tall, splendid specimen of an American, the black decathlon champion, Rafer Johnson, carried the flag, and the bands played "The Star Spangled Banner." It was a moving experience, even though Wilma Rudolph, the black athlete who won three gold medals at Rome, could not hope to buy a hamburger in a dime store in Nashville. It was an experience that congealed for Shirley all of her notions about love of country. "For the first time I knew what it meant to be an American, and I was proud."

Isabel Daniels

In 1956, the Tigerbelles won their second AAU outdoor national championship. That year, an Olympic year, 6 Tigerbelles tried out for the U.S. women's team, and all 6 won places on it. In 1957, at the outdoor nationals, the Tigerbelles had 6 girls out of 6 in the finals of the 200 meters. In all three of these events Tigerbelles ran first, second, and third. In 1958 10 girls had scholarships on the Tigerbelle team. Each of the 10 qualified for a place on the U.S. women's team to the Pan-American Games in Brazil.

Between 1956 and 1958, the Tennessee State Tigerbelle team had strength in depth, and in addition to the four girls who ran the relay team at Rome there was one other star who added to that strength. She was Isabel Daniels, who came to Tennessee State in 1954 and left in 1959, before the trials for the Rome Olympic Games. Isabel was a power runner. She had quick reflexes and was off like a flash at the sound of the starter's gun. Her spikes literally made sparks when her feet hit the ground. She was almost unbeatable at 50 yards or 50 meters, and she held the indoor championship

Isabel Daniels, right (92), of the United States wins the women's 60-meter dash at the Pan American Games at Chicago, Illinois' Soldier's Field on August 29, 1959. Tied for second place are Barbara Jones (95) and Carlotta Gooden of Panama, left (80). Martha Hudson, second from right, finished fourth. AP/Wide World photo.

at these distances in 1956, 1957, 1958, and 1959. She set an indoor world record in the 50-yard dash at Cleveland in 1957.

Isabel was a Georgia farm girl, the youngest of nine children. Her father, a better-off-than-usual farmer, grew corn, tobacco, peanuts, and cotton. "I did pick some cotton," Isabel said, "but before I was big enough to do any good they had cotton-picking machines and peanut shakers." But as a child, she had fun riding one of her father's six horses. Isabel's brother, the one closest to her in age, nicknamed her "Tweety." He said her quick musical voice reminded him of a bird going "tweet-tweet." It was a name that stuck with her during her years as a Tiger-belle.

Like other farm children, Isabel often ran about without shoes. She ran her first race at the Tuskegee Relays barefoot and won. It was at Tuskegee that she was noticed by Coach Temple. He asked her to come to Tennessee State. This brought about a break in family tradition since three older

Daniels children were already attending Florida A&M College. But she accepted Temple's invitation and never regretted it.

At the 1954 outdoor AAU nationals meet in Harrisburg, Pennsylvania, Isabel was on the winning Tennessee State relay team in the 800 meters. She and Lucinda Williams teamed with two former Olympians, Mae Faggs and Cynthia Thompson. Isabel, Lucinda, Mae, and Martha Hudson composed the winning 400-meter relay team at Ponca City in 1955. That was the year she also represented the United States in the Pan-American Games at Mexico City and won a silver medal for a second-place finish in the 60-yard dash.

In 1956 she qualified for a place on the U.S. women's Olympic team and went to Melbourne where she ran fourth in the 100-meter dash and was also on the 400-meter relay team, which placed third.

Tweety Daniels won a place on the U.S. women's team which toured Europe in 1958. She won gold medals for winning 400-meter relays in Moscow, Warsaw, Budapest, and Athens. In 1959 she won another gold medal on the relay team in the Pan-American Games in Chicago. Her track career ended in 1959, and she left the Tigerbelle team that was to perform so brilliantly at Rome in 1960.

Iris Davis

Iris Davis was a member of the U.S. team at the 1972 Munich Olympics and ran on the 400-meter relay team that finished fourth. She also placed fourth on the 100-meter dash, with a time of 11.32 seconds.

Dr. Evie Dennis

In 1976 Dr. Evie Dennis became the first black woman officer of the USOC.

Diane Dixon

Diane Dixon was a member of the U.S.A.'s team to the 1988 Olympics in Seoul, South Korea. She won a silver medal as a member of the 1600-meter relay team. She had been a member of the 1984 1600-meter relay team that qualified the United States to compete in the event, but she did not run in the final. The U.S. team won a gold medal and set a new Olympic record. Dixon, a graduate of Brooklyn's Tech High School, once failed a physical education class.

Mae Faggs

They called her Little Mae because she was so small, only 5 feet 2 inches tall and about 100 pounds. But no more explosive ball of dynamite has ever run on an American track. In 10 years of competition she held every American sprint record, indoors and outdoors, as well as running anchor on world and American record breaking relay teams.

Mae Faggs belongs in the ranks of the immortals of American women's track and field. But she might not have gotten there if it hadn't been for an Irish New York cop named John Brennan of the Police Athletic League (PAL). She was a wiry little nut-brown girl who could not have been much over 10 years old; he was a tall white policeman looking for boys to join the PAL's track and field team.

This is Mae speaking:

> When I was in elementary school a policeman came to school—I think I was in the seventh or eighth grade—and he was looking for some boys to run in a track meet PAL was having from the 111th Precinct, out there in Bayside, Long Island. Naturally, I was interested because I was nothing but a tomboy, anyhow. And we went out in the yard—it was patrolman Dykes at the time—and the boys were running; and I happened to look up at him and I said "Patrolman Dykes, I can beat every one of those boys running out there." He said, "You can?" and I said, "Yeah." He said, "Let's see." And so he lined up some boys with me and we took off down the school court and I beat 'em. He said, "Very good, but the girls don't run until January and we are going to have a little girls' team from the 111th Precinct." And so I joined PAL and ran with him for a little while and after that Sergeant John Brennan decided to start an AAU team from all over the city. That was in 1947. I recall one Sunday he said to me, "Next summer they are going to have the Olympics and you're going to make the Olympic team."

That is how it all began. For the next 10 years through two Olympiads, Sergeant Brennan, the big Irish cop, and Mae Faggs, the tiny black girl, were as close as father and daughter. He was her coach, her mentor, her trusted friend. She was the pride of the PAL, his "ace in the hole" on any relay team in any track meet. He patiently watched her grow in strength and speed. Finally he told her that he felt she was "ready" and that he was going

Mae Faggs and Audrey Patterson at dinner with coaches, aboard the SS *America* on the way to London in 1948. Courtesy K.N. Heinz Photography.

to enter her in the trials of the 1948 U.S. Olympic team to take place in Providence, Rhode Island. They drove in his car from New York to Providence. Mae remembers what happened:

> He told me I was ready and ought to make the Olympic Team. I looked at him and said, "Is that so Mr. Brennan?" and he said "Yeah." And I said, "OK, if you say so. Whatever you say is go with me." Because if Mr. Brennan said I was going to do something, I was going to do it. I had that much faith in him. I remember the first Olympic trials we went to. Mr. Brennan did everything. He taped my feet; gave me my rubdowns. I remember in the 200-meter finals: I was digging my holes—I didn't bother with starting blocks then—and I took off my sweats and the starter said, "OK let's make our marks." All of a sudden I just stood up and I walked off the track—I was just fourteen at the time—and I walked over to Mr. Brennan and I said, "Mr. Brennan, I can't do it." He said, "Wait a minute; you come here," and he just talked to me for a few minutes—I don't think it was over two or three minutes. What he said I can't remember, but what he said to me at the time was just enough to give me the confidence that I needed. I walked back out on the track and I was ready. All the way back home I kept asking Mr. Brennan, "Have I really made the Olympic Team?" and he said, "Yes, you've made it."

She had made the team, but just barely. Mae had been third in the finals behind two rangy experienced athletes, Audrey Patterson of Tennessee State, who was indoor national champion in the 200 meters that year, and Nell Jackson, captain of the Tuskegee team, who had run anchor on the winning 440-yard relay teams in both the indoor and outdoor AAU national meets in 1948. But third place was good enough to make the U.S. Olympic team. She was its youngest member.

Now she would leave Sergeant Brennan, her mother and father, and a brother, who had made the all-city high school basketball team, behind, and sail off to London and the fourteenth Olympiad.

The Faggs family was a poor family, so there was a noticeable difference between her modest New York home and the first-class lounge of the SS *America*, where the actress Hildegarde entertained the U.S. Olympic team. The food was better too. In between meals Mae would munch on pieces of hard candy she took from a jar that was always with her. She was just a bouncy teenager whom nothing phased. The transatlantic trip was fun, and she saw John Brennan's broad Irish smile ahead of her on every wave.

London's Wembley Stadium, with 100,000 spectators and 5,000 athletes from 58 countries, was a spectacle to dazzle even the most mature athletes. Mae was dauntless, even when they placed her in the same 200-meter trial heat with a 30-year-old Dutch girl, Fanny Blankers-Koen, who was to win four gold medals in this Olympiad, and with French runner Louise Spreckles, a seasoned veteran. In the finals of this event Blankers-Koen came in first, and Spreckles finished second. Mae ran third and was eliminated. The loss did not dampen her spirits:

> I remember when it was all over. I pulled up my starting blocks, put on my sweats; I had a little green hat I put on top of my head and I stood there in this big, big doorway and looked around the stadium. I said to myself "I'll be back." The other girls thought I was some place crying, but I was sitting at a little stand drinking hot chocolate and eating cookies. I wasn't a bit concerned that I didn't make it. I just knew I would be back.

After the 1948 Olympics, Alice Coachman told Mae, "You're just beginning. Young as you are, you can be in two or three Olympic Games." Excited by her London experiences, confident of her future, she came back to Bayside, her family the PAL, and of course the ubiquitous Sergeant Brennan.

In 1949, at 15, Mae had her first chance to run in the AAU national indoor meet. She was the mainstay of the PAL's 440-yard relay team and was entered in the 220-yard run, where she would have to face Stella Walsh, who had held the record in the event since 1930, and Audrey Patterson, of Tennessee State, who had placed third in the 200 meters in the London Olympiad. PAL coach Brennan was hopeful. As Mae tells it: "Mr. Brennan said, 'Well, Toots, you ought to be very good in this meet; as a matter of fact I am expecting you to take first place in the 220.' And I said, 'Mr. Brennan, do you really think I'll be able to do it? They are so much bigger than I am. You know, Audrey Patterson is sort of tall and Stella Walsh is bigger and taller.'"

She did what Sergeant Brennan said she could. She beat both Stella Walsh and Audrey Patterson. She set a new American record of 25.8 seconds.

In 1949 and in each succeeding year through 1952 she ran anchor on the PAL's winning 440-yard relay team at AAU indoor nationals; she kept her 220-yard title. From 1950 through 1952, she ran anchor on the 440-yard medley relays. She had picked up the torch in sprints where Alice Coachman had left it.

But she was not the only black girl who had been inspired by Alice Coachman's Olympic gold medal. Nell Jackson, of Tuskegee, who had been on the 1948 Olympic team, was 200-meter outdoor champion in 1949 and 1950 and a member of the U.S. team in the Pan-American Games in 1951. Tennessee State had produced an outstanding sprinter in the 100 and 200 meters. She was Jean Patterson, a former basketball star of Nashville's Pearl High School. Jean had proved her worth by winning gold medals in these two events at the first Pan-American Games in Santiago, Chile; she had won the AAU outdoor national championship in the 200 meters in 1951.

Then there was Mary McNabb of Enterprise, Alabama, the first of the outstanding track stars coached by Marion Armstrong-Perkins at Howard High School in Atlanta. Mary was a reluctant runner, but the spirit of competition soon changed that. Recalling one of her early track experiences, she said:

> One of the exciting races which stands out in my mind was when my high school track team appeared at the Fort Valley meet. We needed to win the relay in order to win the meet. The girl from Booker T. Washington High School got the baton and was so far ahead of me that Mrs. Perkins began to leave the field. She told me later that she began hearing so much cheering until she decided to turn and see what was happening. When she turned I was even with the girl from Booker Washington and luckily I beat her and we won the meet. After that I just found myself liking to run more and more.

Always looking for good runners, Major Cleveland Abbott, coach of the Tuskegee Institute track team, was not long in finding Mary McNabb and persuading her to come to Tuskegee. There she could train with a number of outstanding athletes, AAU champions like Catherine Johnson, Evelyn Lawler, and Nell Jackson, who had been her relay teammates on the 400-meter team. Nell Jackson helped her with her slow starts. "I was known as the major's pet," says Mary. "Whenever something went wrong, I was always elected to face the major."

At the AAU outdoor nationals in Waterbury, Connecticut, in 1951, Mary, then a 17-year-old freshman at Tuskegee, made track history. She won six gold medals, three on the first day in the junior events and three on the second day in the senior events. The Alabama youngster actually ran 14 races to capture five titles in addition to running a heat and a final race with the winning Tuskegee relay team. She ran the finals in the junior 50 meters and 200 meters within 15 minutes of each other. She tied Alice Coachman's 1944 record in the 50 meters and in the 200 meters clipped one-tenth of a second off the world record, established in 1935 by Helen Stephens, the American Olympic star. She was the highest scorer in the meet with 20 points, ahead of Stella Walsh, who scored 18. She was awarded the James M. Roche trophy as the meet's outstanding athlete.

The Waterbury meet was not a good one for Mae Faggs. She had run fifth in the 100 meters behind Mary McNabb, Catherine Hardy of Fort Valley, Jean Patton of Tennessee State, and Janet Moreau of the Providence, Rhode Island Red Diamond Athletic Club, and just ahead of Nell Jackson. Her PAL relay team ran third behind two Tuskegee teams.

In 1951 Catherine Hardy, of Fort Valley, Georgia, ran second to Mary McNabb in the women's division 50 meters and 100 meters events. In 1952, this shy 22-year-old 100-pound sprinter duplicated Mary's 1951 feat by winning three gold medals in the 50 meters, 100 meters, and 200 meters. Like Mary, she tied Alice Coachman's American record in the 50 meters.

And as if these track stars were not enough, there was a 15-year-old from Chicago named Barbara Jones who was beginning to make her meteoric climb to sprint supremacy.

For Mae Faggs it had become clear that it was not going to be easy to fulfill Alice Coachman's prediction. The road to the 1952 Olympic Games in Helsinki, Finland, was going to be rocky. But she wasn't the type to brood over defeats; she had proved that in London. She knew how to snap back. At Buffalo's Connecticut Street Armor in March 1952, she anchored the PAL relay team to wins in the 440-yard relay and the 440-yard medley relay, won the 220-yard dash, and tied the indoor record in the 100-yard dash to win four gold medals. In the 1952 Olympic trials she came in first in the 100 meters, followed by Janet Moreau and Catherine Hardy. She placed second in the 200 meters, this time trailing Hardy. She was the only member of the 1948 Olympic team who won a place on the 1952 team which competed in Helsinki, Finland.

If Mae had survived the grueling tests, others had not. Nell Jackson decided not to compete in the trials. Jean Patton had a leg injury which prevented her from competing. Mary McNabb pulled a leg muscle before the AAU national outdoor meet, tried to run anyway, but only exacerbated her condition. At the trials she was unable to compete. However, because she was such an outstanding athlete, the U.S. Olympic Committee placed her on the team, and she traveled with it but did not run.

There was one thing the U.S. women's international track-and-field team could usually count on before every international meet—a prediction of defeat by the *New York Times*. In 1952 the *Times* prophesied: "The United States is not expected to do much in women's track, in which the Russians are very strong." And it must be admitted that the girls did much to support the prophecy. Mabel Landry, the best American broad jumper of that time, qualified with a leap that broke the previous Olympic record, but in the finals her best jump won seventh place. Catherine Hardy was eliminated in the 100 meters, Mae Faggs in the 200. Americans failed to qualify in the high jump, javelin, and shot put. In the 100-meter finals, Mae came in sixth in competition which included Marjorie Jackson, the winner from Australia, and the veteran from the 1948 Olympics, Fanny Blankers-Koen. And there stood the U.S. Women's Olympic Track Team with no medals and a team score of exactly one point, contributed by Mae Faggs.

Spirits were low. There seemed little hope for the American team in the relays. Members of the team had never run together. Janet Moreau was from Providence; Catherine Hardy from Fort Valley, Georgia; Barbara Jones from Chicago; and Mae from New York. Worse still, Barbara Jones, the 15-year-old, wouldn't practice.

Perhaps more than anything else, passing the baton is the key to a winning relay team. Runners must have the assurance that when a teammate passes the baton, they will be able to grasp it without stopping to look back; she must have the same faith. This comes from working and hours of practice. Split-second accuracy in baton passing makes a difference.

Mae took charge. Helsinki was rainy and cold, but the team practiced every day. Mae used coercion with Barbara; she would refuse to do Barbara's hair if the girl from Chicago would not come out for practice. Mae told Barbara: "If you can't come out and train with us and get this stick passing right, then I am not going to set your hair."

Australia was supposed to win the relay. Its team included the double gold-medal winner Marjorie Jackson. She had run the 100 meters in the very fast time of 11.5 seconds. England and Germany also had impressive and powerful teams.

The relay was run on an oval, and this necessitated staggered lanes. Mae ran the first leg, and to her discomfiture, she was placed in a lane in front of the Australian girl. She was determined not to let her pass. Everything was at stake. All of their critics were saying the American girls were cream puffs and couldn't stand up to international competition.

Mae kept ahead of the competition and passed the baton to Barbara Jones with a lead of almost two yards. Barbara held the lead and added possibly another yard. Janet Moreau ran third and lost ground. When she handed the baton to Catherine Hardy, Australia, England, and Germany had moved ahead, in that order. Then the U.S. team saw the importance of all their practice; Marjorie Jackson of Australia dropped the baton.

England, Germany, and the United States passed the Australian team. Catherine caught the German runner 30 yards from the finish line and passed the English athlete just 2 yards from the tape, winning by a stride. The American team had won 10 points and four glistening gold medals. But they had done something more: They had set a new world record of 45.9 seconds. They were not cream puffs.

In the middle of the stadium three American black girls and one American white girl put their arms around each other and danced jubilantly in a circle. They laughed and screamed until their eyes filled with tears of joy.

On the way home, the American team competed in the British Empire Games, held at London's White City Stadium. Mae had kept her promise to come back. On the American team Dorothy Dwyer of Brooklyn, New York, had replaced Barbara Jones. Marjorie Jackson and Winsome Cripps of Australia teamed with two South African girls, Daphne Hasenjager and Edna Maskell, to make up a British Empire team. The British team won the 880-meter relay, and Marjorie Jackson gained redemption for dropping the baton at Helsinki. The winning team set a new record but could not claim it because of its mixed international composition. The second-place time of the American team was also record breaking, and it was offered for acceptance.

During the next four years, Mae Faggs became a legend, but not without heartache that was almost impossible to bear. She left the PAL and went to college at Tennessee State University. Friends had arranged for her to receive a work scholarship. Now, with the little help her parents could give her, she could finish college, become a teacher, get married, and have four sons, in that order. That was her ambition.

When she arrived at Tennessee State, the status of women's track was poor. There was little interest among students or the university administration. Indeed, there were just two girls on the team, Mae and Cynthia Thompson, a 31-year-old woman who had been a member of the 1948 and 1952 Jamaican Olympic teams. Cynthia had left Jamaica, gone to London, and now had come to the United States determined to satisfy her ambition to become a physician. She planned to go to Meharry Medical College in Nashville, but before she could do this, she had to earn her undergraduate degree, so she entered nearby Tennessee State.

Moreover, there was no money for travel to track meets. That first year Mae learned to her bitter astonishment that the school did not have money to pay her expenses to the AAU national meet so that she could defend her title in the 220-yard dash, which she had held since 1949. Just one meet, at Tuskegee, was all the competition either runner had, and the school's officials seriously considered eliminating women's track altogether. This was seven years before Tennessee State University gave the American Olympic team Wilma Rudolph.

That women's track was not abandoned at Tennessee State was due more to Mae Faggs than any other individual. If the Tuskegee meet was the only opportunity to run, then she would win all the sprint events in the meet. She was more than an individual star; she had team spirit and demanded the same from her teammates. Her years of experience had taught her that even the best track athlete could take nothing for granted in practice or in competition. She was the glue that kept the team in peak condition and at its competitive best.

Things got better in 1954. Other students came out for track, among them two freshmen—Isabel Daniels of Jakin, Georgia, and Lucinda Williams from Bloomingdale, Georgia. Isabel was a power runner. Like a coiled spring, she exploded from her starting blocks. She charged down the track with so much physical force that her spikes struck sparks. Lucinda was a more relaxed runner but just as fast. For four years the two of them were to seesaw back and forth for sprint supremacy. The two younger students teamed with Mae and Cynthia to form the Tennessee State 800-meter relay team which ran in the AAU outdoor nationals in Harrisburg, Pennsylvania, that year. They set a new American record, and Mae won the 220-yard run.

The AAU indoor nationals for 1955 were held in Chicago. This gave the Chicago Comets, a team sponsored by the Catholic Youth Organization (CYO) and coached by Joseph Robichaux, an opportunity to compete in full force. At stake in this meet were not only indoor championship titles but a place for the winners on the U.S. team to the Pan-American Games, which were to be held in Mexico City in March of that year.

Just as the PAL had fielded an interracial track team which developed runners like Mae Faggs and Patricia Monsanto, a javelin thrower, so the CYO on the South Side had ignited the spark which attracted black and white female athletes in Chicago. Both in New York and Chicago the athletic programs gave awkward teenage girls purpose and incentive to achieve. On the Comets team were such outstanding athletes as Mabel Landry, the broad jumper, and Barbara Jones, the sprinter who had been on the 1952 Olympic team. Alfrances Lyman and Margaret Mathews were two other promising stars. With the exception of Mabel Landry, all of these athletes went to Tennessee State in 1956.

At the indoor nationals the Chicago Comets won both the 440-yard relay and 440-yard medley. Barbara Jones, now 18, beat Mae Faggs in the 100-yard dash; Alfrances Lyman defeated Stella Walsh in the 220-yard dash. For Isabel Daniels, the Chicago meet was a landmark too. For the first time, she beat her team captain, Mae Faggs. Her tremendous burst of power carried her to the tape ahead of Mae in the 60-yard dash. But it did more than that; it gave her the self-confidence to know that she could beat Mae if she really tried. She never stopped trying after that.

In Mexico City, in the 60-meter dash, Mae beat Bertha Diaz of Cuba in the first heat in 7.5 seconds, and Isabel beat Daisy DeCastro of Brazil in the same fast time. In the finals, however, Diaz beat them both, Isabel taking second and Mae finishing fifth. In the 100 meters both Mae and Barbara Jones set new Pan-American records in their trial heats. In the finals Barbara beat Mae for first place and set an even faster record, 11.5 seconds. In the 400-meter relay, Mabel Landry and Barbara Jones teamed with Mae and Isabel to win the event. For the first time in a long time, it was clear that Mae had challengers worthy of her speed.

Of course, not every challenger was lucky enough to rob Mae of a gold medal. There was Jo Ann Baker, a tall, well-built athlete who came to Tennessee State from Indianapolis. The first day she stepped on the practice track she asked, "Where is Mae Faggs?" and when Mae was pointed out to her, she asked, "That little thing can run?" Mae was not long in answering her question. In one race she left Jo Ann so far behind that Jo Ann never asked the question again.

With many an athlete, especially one who had already been on two Olympic teams, defeats by younger runners at Chicago and Mexico City would have had a dampening effect. Not so with Mae. For the AAU outdoor nationals at Ponca City, Oklahoma, she trained as if her life depended on it. Again and again she practiced her starts—how to lean into the tape at the finish and how to finish strong. Hard work paid off. The reward for Mae in 1955 and for the Tennessee State team she captained was a cornucopia of gold medals. At Ponca City, Mae took Stella Walsh's record in the 100-yard dash, a record that had stood for 25 years, since 1930. Mae ran the 100-yard dash in 10.7 and set a new meet record in the 220-yard dash, wiping out Stella Walsh's other record. To crown that, she ran anchor on Tennessee State's 440-yard relay team, which clocked the fastest time ever run in the United States, 49.1 seconds. Another 25-year-old record set by the Melrose Athletic Club was broken. Mae was high point scorer of that meet.

Tennessee State was high point scorer in both the girls' and women's divisions at the Ponca City meet. Contributing to the victory was a tiny runner, even smaller than Mae, 4-feet-10-inch Martha Hudson of Marietta, Georgia. It never dawned on Martha that there was anything unusual about her outrunning girls whose legs were almost twice as long as hers. She had run with Mae, Isabel Daniels, and Lucinda Williams in the record breaking relay, and then had set a new record in the junior division 75-yard dash. Tennessee State won all four places in this event. Lucinda Williams was second; Joe Ann Baker placed third; and in fourth place was a tall beanstalk of a girl named Wilma Rudolph. Wilma fared better in the 100-yard dash, taking second place behind Isabel Daniels. And Isabel, still invincible in short distances because of her explosive starts, won the 50-yard dash in the junior division record breaking time of 5.8 seconds.

Ponca City was a turning point for Tennessee State. It began an ascendancy in women's track and field which was seldom challenged. Tuskegee was eclipsed. Its coach, Major Cleveland Abbott, died that year, and with his passing went much of the drive and inspiration that made the school preeminent in women's track for so many years.

Tennessee State had developed a summer program for promising high school athletes. Isabel Daniels and Lucinda had first come to the summer training school while they were high school students. Wilma Rudolph and Martha Hudson were still high school students when they ran on the Tennessee State team at Ponca City and later in the 1956 outdoor nationals. Soon the school had several waves of promising athletes coming in, one generation after another.

But the bright star for these cohorts was still Mae Faggs. Mae went to Africa in 1956. She was chosen by the U.S. State Department as the only woman athlete to accompany six outstanding male stars on a goodwill tour to Monrovia, Liberia, Accra, the Gold Coast (now Ghana), and Lagos and Ibada in Nigeria. Having paid her the signal honor of choosing her to represent all American women athletes, it never occurred to the State Department that its choice was as poor as Job's turkey. Mae needed a coat. Usually if she needed a nice dress or coat to look presentable at some important affair, she could count on borrowing it from one of the girls in her dormitory. But for a 14,000-mile trip such a loan was not possible. A local Nashville merchant, when told of her plight, cut the sales price of one of his coats in half. That is how Mae went off to represent the United States looking chic and well-dressed.

The first track meet for Tennessee State in 1956 was the AAU indoor nationals, sponsored by the now defunct *Washington Evening Star* in Washington, D.C., held in the National Guard Armory.

Having beaten Mae in the 60-yard dash in Chicago and in Mexico City the year before, Isabel Daniels now came on to beat her in the 100-yard dash. Isabel equaled the indoor world record set by Jean Patton in 1951 and equaled by Mae in 1952. She also won the 50-yard dash, tying her own outdoor record at this distance and clipping two-tenths of a second off the 26-year-old record of Stella Walsh. The press called her "this nation's leading hope for the Women's Olympic sprint events."

Mae had no alibi. When you beat her, you did so because you were the better runner. She took defeat like a champion. When she was beaten by one of her younger teammates, she seemed almost glad that her will to win had rubbed off on the victor. After Isabel had beaten her, she remained undaunted. Isabel and Mae, running third and fourth leg on the Tennessee relay team, made up a 10-yard deficit and won the relay with a 5-yard lead.

Of course, Mae never stayed beaten. The outdoor nationals took place that year in the University of Pennsylvania's stadium in Philadelphia. A searing 95-degree heat scorched the track, but Mae was unbeatable. The headline on the sports page of the *Washington Evening Star* read:

Mae Faggs Steals Show
In Women's AAU Track

She won gold medals in the 100-yard dash and the 220-yard dash, and as anchor of the 440-yard relay. Isabel was second in the 100, Wilma Rudolph in the 220. Isabel took a gold medal in the 50-yard dash, just nosing out Barbara Jones and Lucinda Williams who ran almost a dead heat with her. Good sprinters were springing up all around, but Mae Faggs, at 24, was still the unquestioned Queen of the Sprints.

The next week, the Olympic trials took place in Washington, D.C. Olympic trials are always a tough endeavor for the American athlete. There is always the fear of a disqualifying injury, always the risk of becoming too tense, always the chance that some rank outsider will run the race or jump the jump of her life and outstrip the seasoned veteran.

There was just one chance to make the team. The athlete had to meet international standards for the event and be first or second in the finals. Past performances did not count. This is why Barbara Jones, who had run on the world record breaking U.S. relay team as a 15-year-old in Helsinki, failed to make the team in 1956. She had set a new meet record in the 100 meters at the Pan-American Games and won the national indoor title in the 100 in 1955. At the outdoor nationals in Philadelphia, she had been beaten in the 50-yard dash by Isabel, but only after she had set a new meet record of 6.3 seconds in a trial heat. One of the all-time greats among American sprinters, she did not meet the crucial test for the Olympic team.

Mae went into the Olympic trials with a half-dozen young sprinters snapping at her heels, but she came through and brought her teammates with her. Isabel beat her for first place in the 100-meter run; Mae took second. In the 200-meter run both she and Wilma Rudolph survived the trials and entered the finals together. Wilma, or "Skeeter," was a bundle of raw nerves, but it was Mae who steadied her nerves and kept her in the race.

Both Mae and Wilma tied the American record of 24.1 seconds, but Mae won first place by the barest margin. It might have been different. Mae said: "We were running around a turn, and as we came off the turn, Skeeter was in front of me. But she turned to look back, and when she did, I beat her to the tape by just inches. And I said to her afterwards, 'Skeeter, as long as you live, don't you ever look back in a race again.' And she never did."

When Tennessee State's campaign was over in that Olympic trial, six of its athletes had made the Olympic team. Thus Mae, who had been the only member of the 1948 team to make the 1952 team, became the only member of the 1952 team to make the 1956 team. Alice Coachman's prophecy was becoming truer and truer.

Nell Jackson of Tuskegee was coach of the U.S. Women's Olympic Track and Field Team. She had been an American champion in the 200 meters and was a member of the 1948 U.S. team to the Pan-American Games in 1951. She was the first black woman to coach a women's Olympic track-and-field team.

The 1956 team trained for two weeks and then flew to Melbourne. Except for Mae, the trip was a new experience for the team of girls 17 to 19. They flew to Honolulu, to the Fiji Islands, to Okinawa, and then to Melbourne. High in the sky Wilma Rudolph was too nervous to eat, but not her teammate Mae. At each meal she would finish and then help Skeeter finish hers. It was an act of love.

Melbourne was cold and rainy, and things did not go as expected for the American team in either sprints or field events. In the 100 meters, Mae was eliminated in the first heat, which was won by Australian champion Betty Cuthbert, the final winner of the event. Lucinda Williams was eliminated in the second heat. Isabel Daniels, who survived to the finals, ran fourth. In the 200 meters Wilma was eliminated in her trial heat, and Mae in the semifinals. When it came time to run the relays, the morale of the American team was low.

It got no better in the morning trials. The team was not working well together; they lacked confidence in themselves and each other. Nobody was doing what she was supposed to do. As Mae told it,

> After qualifying heats in the morning, Skeeter was upset. She thought she had run out of the passing zone. Margaret and Isabel were down in the dumps because of our slow time. So I took all of them to the warm-up track in back of the stadium, and I said some terrible words to them. I told them I didn't know what they were going to do, but I was going to have me a medal. I said I didn't come all this distance just to go home empty-handed. I am going to have me a medal. Now how was I going to win something without the other three? But I pitched one back there. I had to, because they had lost all confidence in themselves. I told them "You'd better move. I'm not playing with you."

Australia won the relay with the fastest Olympic time ever recorded, but an all–Tennessee State team came in third, even though Margaret Mathews was a last-minute replacement for the athlete originally scheduled to run.

And that was the beginning of the Tigerbelles, who were to write such a brilliant page in the history of relays in the years that followed. Mae got her medal, a bronze to go with the gold she won at Helsinki. And Wilma Rudolph won her first Olympic medal.

Mae Faggs' track career was over. She had been a front-rank competitor for more than 10 years. She had medals, ribbons, and shelves full of silver cups. She held records, indoor and outdoor, in the 100-yard and 220-yard runs; in the 60-yard, 100-yard, and 200-yard dashes; and on relay teams which held world and American records in the 400 meters, 440 yards, and 880 meters. She had competed in London, Helsinki, Melbourne, Mexico City, and coached track in Africa. And she was only 24. Quite a record for a tiny little brown girl whose mother named her Aeriwentha Mae Faggs. Mae had done more than establish a personal record. She had laid the foundation for the future of the Tennessee State University women's track team.

Records are made to be broken; better training conditions and increased competition make this inevitable. Since Mae Faggs' day there have been faster runners but no one who better deserves the title Queen of the Sprints.

Mable Ferguson

In 1972, at Munich, Mable Ferguson won a silver medal as a member of the U.S.A.'s second-place 1600-meter relay team and placed fifth in the 400-meter run. She held national titles in the 220- and 400-yard dashes.

Barbara Ferrell

At Mexico City in 1968, Barbara Ferrell was a member of the 400-meter relay team that finished first, setting an Olympic and world record of 42.8 seconds. She won a silver medal that year in the 100-meter dash with a second-place time of 11.1 seconds.

Gail Fitzgerald

Gail Fitzgerald competed in the pentathlon in Munich in 1972 and in Montreal in 1976, but did not win a medal.

Benita Fitzgerald-Brown

Benita Fitzgerald-Brown won a gold medal in the 100-meter hurdles in the 1984 Los Angeles Olympics with a time of 12.8 seconds.

Kim Gallagher

In 1984, at the Los Angeles Olympiad, Kim Gallagher won a silver medal in the 800-meter run.

Missy Gerald

Missy Gerald ran in the 800-meter run at the 1984 Los Angeles Olympics. She also competed in the 100-meter hurdles, but she failed to make the finals.

Randy Givens

Randy Givens competed in the 200-meter dash at the 1984 Los Angeles Olympics, placing sixth. Her teammates, Valerie Brisco-Hooks and Florence Griffith-Joyner, finished first and second.

Florence Griffith-Joyner

Florence Griffith-Joyner, "Flo Jo" as she is known affectionately to millions of adoring fans, has brought fashion, flair, and high finance to women's track. She has done more than any other woman to glamorize the image of America's female track stars. And unlike most of her earlier predecessors, who gained only trophies, ribbons, medals, and worldwide acclaim for their track exploits, Florence Griffith-Joyner has earned nearly $4 million. "Cash Flo" is another of her nicknames.

Florence Griffith-Joyner raises her arms in victory as she sweeps first across the finish line to win the gold medal in the women's 100-meter final at the 1988 Seoul Olympics. Her time of 10.4 seconds broke her own Olympic record. AP/Wide World photo.

She started her athletic career as a Cinderella girl, but because Olympic athletes are now allowed to be paid for personal appearances and product endorsements, her carriage did not turn into a pumpkin when the Olympic applause stopped. The race she has run against poverty has been as swift and successful as the races she ran against athletic competitors.

Before the U.S. Olympic trials in July 1988, Florence beat the previous world record of 10.76 seconds in the 100-meter dash four times. The first mark was disallowed because of a helping wind, but she ran the races in 10.60, 10.49, 10.71, and 10.61 seconds, respectively, claiming the title of the World's Fastest Woman.

With her shoulder-length hair, meticulous makeup, one-legged running tights, lace-trimmed bikini briefs, and long multicolored fingernails, she has run into the record books, a rainbow blur of blazing color. "Looking good is almost as important as running well," she said.

At the Seoul Summer Olympics in Korea in September 1988, she won three gold medals in the 100- and 200-meter races and the 400-meter relay, and a silver medal in the 1600-meter relay. With these four Olympic medals, three gold and one silver, she surpassed Wilma Rudolph's record of three gold medals set in Rome in 1960 and just missed tying the record of Fanny Blankers-Koen of Holland, who won four gold medals in women's track and field in the 1948 Olympics.

The first races Florence Griffith-Joyner ran were not against fleet-footed competitors on a cinder track. They were against swift jackrabbits on the coarse, dry sands of the Mojave Desert. "Out of all of them, maybe we caught one or two," she remembered. In 1963, when Florence was 4, her mother separated from her father and moved with her 11 children from their house in the southern California desert to the Jordan Downs housing project in Watts, a section of Los Angeles that was to be scarred by riots. It was during summer visits to her father's house in the desert that she competed against the jackrabbits, honing the skills that would soon earn her the title the World's Fastest Woman.

Delorez Florence Griffith was born December 21, 1959, the seventh of 11 children. Her father was an electronics technician, her mother a seamstress. She remembers the days in Los Angeles. In 1989 she told a reporter, "There were days we didn't have food; there were days when we had oatmeal for breakfast, lunch and dinner, but my mother always figured it out." Her mother, who was also named Florence, called her "Dee Dee" because she didn't want "name confusion" in the home.

Florence's mother was 20 when she left her parents and one young son behind in rural North Carolina and went to California, "the land of opportunity," she said. "I thought I had a chance to be a model, that's what I wanted to be. That dream faded away."

At 7, Florence began running. In elementary and high school she competed in the 50- and 70-meter dashes with the Sugar Ray Robinson Youth Foundation, a program for underprivileged youth.

At 14 she won the annual Jesse Owens National Youth Games and a trip to a San Francisco track meet. She won the same meet the following year, but that victory brought disappointment. Jesse Owens was there and congratulated her on the victory and her promising track career, and then he gave Florence the bad news. He told Florence that the rules would not allow her to compete in the sectional competition in Texas because she had won the year before. "I had never been out of California and I wanted to go," she said. "I started to cry and said, 'I don't like that man.' I found out later who Jesse Owens was."

Her passion for colorful running outfits may have been inspired by a pet boa constrictor she owned as a high school student. The snake was named Brandy, and when it shed, she saved the skins and painted them different colors. Her penchant for pursuits like knitting, crocheting, and styling hair and fingernails also played a part in the colorful self-designed sports clothes that were to become her athletic trademark.

She graduated from Los Angeles' Jordan High School in 1978; she had set school records in sprinting and the long jump. The following fall she enrolled at California State University at Northridge where she wanted to major in business. But during her freshman year she did not have money for tuition and books, so she dropped out of college and took a job as a bank teller. Bob Kersee, an assistant track coach at California State, wanted to see her continue her academic and athletic careers. He helped her apply for financial aid. She returned to school and continued her pursuit of athletic excellence.

Bob Kersee thought Florence should concentrate on the 200 meters because he felt she did not come out of the starting blocks fast enough to compete successfully at shorter distances. In 1980 Kersee took an assistant coaching position at UCLA and with some reluctance, Florence decided to change schools and join him there. "I had a 3.25 grade point average in business [at Cal State Northridge], but UCLA didn't offer my major," she said. "I had to switch to psychology. But my running was starting up, and I knew that Bobby was the best coach for me. So it kind of hurts to say this—I choose athletics over academics."

In the trials for the 1980 Olympics she narrowly missed making the team. She finished fourth behind, among others, Valerie Brisco-Hooks, an old high school rival. The United States boycotted the 1980 Olympics to protest the Soviet Union's invasion of Afghanistan.

But in 1982 Florence became the National Collegiate Athletic Association (NCAA) champion in the 200 meters with a time of 22.39 seconds. The next year she won the NCAA 400 meters and placed second in the 200 meters. She continued to train with Kersee as a member of his World Class Track Club, though she was no longer a UCLA student.

She won a place on the U.S. team for the 1984 Olympics and won a second-place silver medal in the 200 meters with a time of 22.04 seconds, almost a quarter of a second behind Valerie Brisco-Hooks, who won the event in 21.81 seconds.

Feeling the effects of this narrow defeat by her long-time rival, Florence reduced her track activities and took a job as a customer-service representative at the Union Bank in Los Angeles. To supplement her income, she worked nights as a beautician, braiding hair. She gained weight and by 1986 considered herself in semiretirement.

That year she ran the 200 meters one second slower than she had in 1985. Kersee told a reporter that Florence was 60 pounds overweight and was "so wide," he could not tell if she was "coming or going." Florence bristled at Kersee's comment about her weight. She said she had gained only 15 pounds. In 1986 Joyner was all but retired. She wrote poetry and children's books, drew sketches, and designed hair and nails in her flashy mode. "Running is just something else I do with my life," she said.

Early in 1987 Florence decided to renew her athletic career. She asked Kersee to help her train for the 1988 Olympic trials. He agreed, with the stipulation that she would adhere to a rigorous training schedule and work harder than she had ever worked before. She agreed and began a postmidnight schedule of grueling training sessions while continuing to work as a beautician. "It was a time to run better or move on," she told *Chicago Tribune* reporter Phil Hersh. "What did others have that I didn't have?" she recalls. "I studied and realized they didn't have any more. Except they were getting uniforms that said 'USA' and I wasn't."

She received support and encouragement from a new boyfriend, Al Joyner, the triple-jumper who had won the 1984 Olympic gold medal. He was the brother of World Class Track Club teammate Jackie Joyner-Kersee. Florence and Al were married in October 1987 in Las Vegas, Nevada. The couple appeared on television's "Newlywed Game" and won a trip to Jamaica.

Florence Griffith-Joyner reduced to 130 pounds and improved her starts and her speed. She won a silver medal in the 200 meters at the World Championship Games in Rome in the summer of 1987 and then ran the third leg of the 400-meter relay on the U.S. gold medal team. She broke no records but received attention as a perspective top contender in the next Olympics. The *Chicago Tribune* reported on July 22, 1988: "Griffith-Joyner defied heat, humidity and convention by running in a hooded, silver bodysuit that must have been designed for the Olympic speed skating team from Pluto."

Finishing second in the 200 meters in Rome pushed her to improve. "When you've been second best for so long, you can either accept it, or try to become the best," she told a writer for *Ms. Magazine*. "I made the decision to try and be the best in 1988."

She began a regimen of daily track workouts and a weight-lifting program four times a week. She did partial squats with a 320-pound weight on her shoulders. She used her lunch hours at the bank to work out, and in the evenings she earned extra money as a part-time beautician. She often trained until after midnight. By the end of the year, she ranked first in the 200 meters. To get in more training time as the Seoul Olympics approached, Florence left the bank and took a part-time position in employee relations with Anheuser-Busch. Her supervisors were instructed not to watch the time clock too closely, and this gave her more training time.

She concentrated on the 200 meters and added the 100 to her track repertoire. At the Michelob Invitational in San Diego on June 25, 1988, she ran a 10.89 seconds in the 100 meters. That time, her best to that date, prompted her to tell Kersee, "I am ready to break the record."

The U.S. trials for the Seoul Olympiad began on July 16, 1988, at the Indiana University–Purdue University track stadium in Indianapolis. In the first preliminary 100-meter heat, wearing a one-legged, lime-green racing suit, Florence ran a 10.60-second race, breaking the four-year-old record held by Evelyn Ashford. Meet officials ruled that the tailwind of 3.2 meters per hour invalidated the time since the maximum allowable wind speed was 2 meters per hour. In the second round of 100-meter trials, this time wearing a purple one-legged racing suit and a white bikini bottom trimmed with purple, she clocked an amazing 10.49 seconds that eclipsed the world record by more than a quarter of a second. The question of wind speed was raised again because the stadium flags waved briskly, but the wind gauge for the 100 meters registered 0.0. But the gauge for the triple jump read 4.3. The timing experts ruled the angle of the wind in different sections of the stadium could make such a reading possible and legally acceptable.

Bob Kersee was shocked by Florence's time. "No one could envision a 10.49 for a woman in the 100," he told a *Chicago Tribune* reporter. "I am still shocked about it because I hadn't told her to run fast yet," he said after the race. Kersee predicted Florence would return to the stadium the following day, win the 100- and 200-meter races, and break the world records.

The next day, Sunday, July 17, now wearing a black bodysuit with a yellow side stripe, Florence ran against three-time Olympian Evelyn Ashford and others in the semifinal heat. Kersee's strategy was for Florence to run under Ashford's previous time of 10.76. "I wanted her to run 10.71 or 10.72 in the semifinals and 10.50 something in the final," he said. But she won the semifinal heat in 10.70 seconds, beating Ashford by five feet. In the finals, two hours later, now clad in a one-legged blue leotard and a white bikini, she did even better. She won the race in 10.61 seconds to beat Evelyn Ashford by ten feet. In four races over two days she ran the four fastest 100 meters in women's track history with three of the times unaided by the wind.

Later that week she set an American record in the quarter finals of the

200 meters with a time of 21.77 seconds. (The world record was held jointly by two East Germans, Heike Drechsler and Marita Koch.) Joyner took the 200 meters semifinal in 21.90 seconds, wearing a white fishnet bodysuit, and won first place with a time of 21.82 seconds.

Florence's running times were as electrifying as her running outfits. Christine Brennan of the *Washington Post*, characterized Florence as "a Maybelline advertisement waiting to happen. And she knows it." Her long fingernails, painted with orange stripes one day and fuchsia tips the next, were drawing almost as much media attention as her running. She was excluded from an Olympic relay team in 1984 because coaches said her fingernails were too long for passing the baton. Most Olympians would have reached for the nail clippers, but not Florence. She kept her fingernails and her pride, and did not run the race. "She was mad about that," said her sister, Sissy.

Kersee claimed Florence's greater speed came from improved strength and endurance. Florence said she believed her improved performance was the result of a more relaxed running style. She said she believed a runner could attain a greater speed by not trying so hard. "For a long time I thought that being relaxed meant you were running slow, but its the contrary," she told a *People Magazine*'s writer. "When you are trying to go fast, you are fighting against your body instead of letting go."

A few weeks after the Olympic trials Joyner fired Kersee and replaced him with her husband, Al Joyner. She said she needed full-time attention, which Kersee was unable to give her because he was coaching six other athletes. And she claimed Kersee charged her 18.5 percent of her promotional earnings. It was her husband, Al Joyner, not Bob Kersee, who had coached her to run the 10.49 seconds in the 100 meters, she said. "When Bobby was overwhelmed with his responsibilities to other athletes, Al was there to film me, advise me on my form, and encourage me to keep going."

She confided to the late Pete Axthelm of *Newsweek* that she had gone into semiretirement in 1986 because Kersee was charging her too much and that he had tried to keep his wife, Jackie Joyner-Kersee, and Jackie's brother, Al Joyner, apart. She called Kersee's World Class Track Club a "cult" and claimed that one of its members, Valerie Brisco-Hooks, was parentally dependent on Kersee and his wife, Jackie. Bob Kersee publicly denied her allegations.

Florence quickly became a media sensation. Her warm smile, bright eyes, and colorful costumes were splashed across the covers of *Newsweek, Life, Ebony,* and *Jet.* Foreign magazines were also interested in her. *Paris Match* called Florence *la tigresse noire,* the black tigress. *Stern* and *Sports International* published stories about her track success.

That August she ran in two European races—the 100 meters in Malmo,

Sweden, and the 100 meters in Gateshead, England. She commanded $25,000 in appearance money per race, a sharp increase from the $1,500 she had been paid earlier. Florence hired a business manager, Gordon Baskin. "We probably had 200 calls in three days from all over the world," Baskin told the *New York Times*.

Florence received offers from film producers, television, modeling agencies, fashion magazines, and other periodicals, including *Good Housekeeping, Ms.* and *People Magazine*. Her performance in the Olympic trials moved her into the highest earnings bracket for Olympic athletes. And the 1988 Seoul Olympiad was still ahead of her.

Florence spent the week before the Seoul Olympics training at the Nihol Aerobics Center in Japan on an infield track with a rock garden in its median strip. The center's director was so impressed with Florence that he held a Buddhist ceremony in her honor. He said it would increase her athletic powers at Seoul.

The city of Seoul had constructed a magnificent stadium for the Olympic Games, 24.8 miles from what had been the Demilitarized Zone during the Korean War. It refurbished Kimbo International Airport. The streets were meticulously cleaned by enthusiastic old women with pushbrooms. The beat of Korea's traditional dragon drums was heard throughout the city. Florence and her teammates bought souvenirs and silk blouses at the Itaewon Bazaar and ate in the exotic curbside cafés.

At the Olympiad's opening ceremony 1,500 dancers formed the word *o-so-ose-yo*, "welcome." Thousands of balloons went up, and 76 parachutists under canopies as colorful as Florence's running outfits came down in the center of the stadium. White parasols were placed along the green infield to be used by athletes as shields against Seoul's hot autumn sun.

Eighty-eight children born on September 30, 1981, the day Seoul was designated as the city to host the 24th Olympiad, paraded around the stadium in traditional Korean dress. A record 161 nations sent teams to the Olympics, and 250,000 visitors came to watch the 1,700 athletes compete.

At the Seoul Olympiad, Florence continued to rewrite the record books. In the 100 meters she set an Olympic record in the trials with a 10.62-second run, and then, in the finals, she ran the 100 in 10.54 seconds, the second-fastest time ever, and won a gold medal. Competing in the 200 meters four days later, she broke the world record twice—in the semifinals with 21.56 seconds and in the finals with a gold medal–winning time of 21.34 seconds. The previous world record of 21.71 seconds had been set by Marita Koch of East Germany nine years earlier.

Florence, describing how she began the 200-meter race, said she tried to "go hard as I can out of the blocks, make up the staggers on everybody in the turn, stay relaxed and use all I have coming home. I lift and I reach out when I run. I run more like a guy than a girl."

In those two events Joyner, as Pete Axthelm reported in *Newsweek*, might have run faster races. But she "slowed down slightly while well ahead to flash that million dollar smile at the cameras." Recalling the finals for the 100 meters, she told Dick Patrick of *USA Today*, "It hit me right there at fifty. I thought, 'I have the race. I've finally got the gold.' I was so excited I couldn't do anything else but smile." In the 400-meter relay on October 1 Florence won her third gold medal, running the third leg of the race.

Two days before the 1,600-meter relay, the U.S. coaches Terry Crawford and Fred Thompson decided to include Joyner as the race's anchor runner. The United States finished second behind a strong Soviet Union team. The race was run just 40 minutes after Florence had given her brilliant performance in the 400-meter relay. She ran her anchor leg in 48.1 seconds, just behind Olga Bryzgina, who anchored the Soviet team. Florence told a reporter that she treasured the silver medal more than the gold ones. "I felt the silver was a special one, because of the team's trust in giving me the chance. That silver is gold for me."

For the first 92 years of the modern Olympics, questions of politics, money, and amateurism were prominent off-field issues. The 1968 Olympics in Mexico City are remembered for the protest of some black athletes and student demonstrations. The 1972 Munich Olympics were marred by the terrorist murders of 11 Israeli athletes. The 1988 Olympics were clouded by the question of drug use by some of the Olympiad's star performers.

Rumors that some athletes had used anabolic steroids to increase their strength and endurance swept through the Olympic Village. And then, on September 27, the rumors became hard news when the International Olympic Committee's Olympic doping control laboratory reported that Canadian sprinter Ben Johnson, who had just set a world's record in the 100 meters, had traces of anabolic steroids in his urine. Two Bulgarian weight lifters, Mitko Grablev and Angel Gorvchev, who had also won gold medals, were found to have used steroids.

Johnson and the Bulgarians were stripped of their medals and their records and expelled from the Olympic Village because they had violated the Olympic rule against using performance drugs. Seven other athletes also tested positive for steroids and were banned from the games.

Florence Griffith-Joyner and her sister-in-law Jackie Joyner-Kersee were drawn into the performance-drug controversy by a Brazilian athlete who publicly accused them of using steroids. Joaquim Cruz, the Brazilian 800-meter silver medalist, told Brazilian television reporters and a sportswriter for *USA Today* that he believed the two American athletes had used drugs. "In 1984, you could see an extremely feminine person, but today she [Florence Griffith-Joyner] looks more like a man than a woman," Cruz said.

In a subsequent interview Cruz charged that Joyner and Kersee "must be doing something that isn't normal to get all those muscles." When his spurious and illogical allegations received widespread media attention, Cruz claimed reporters had misquoted him.

Florence vehemently denied using steroids. "I was very hurt that someone would say something like that about me and Jackie," she told New York's *Newsday*. "It hurts me, but it didn't bother me. I know that I am a champion. I am not into drugs. Chasing all those records and giving the young kids coming up something to chase, that's what the sport is all about." The test conducted by Olympic medical officers showed no trace of steroids in Florence or Jackie Joyner-Kersee.

In 1988, Florence was named French Sportswoman of the Year and Athlete of the Year by Tass, the Soviet press agency. In 1989 she received the U.S. Olympic Committee award, the Golden Camera award in Berlin, and the Harvard Foundation award for outstanding contributions to society. She also won the 1988 Jesse Owens award as the year's outstanding track-and-field athlete and the 1988 Sullivan award as the top American amateur athlete.

After Seoul, the media's spotlight continued to shine on Florence. She appeared on the David Letterman, Arsenio Hall and Larry King television talk shows, and she made a guest appearance in an episode of the NBC sitcom, "227." Comedian Bob Hope invited her to appear on his Christmas show with the All-American Champs.

Florence has received lucrative business and advertising offers. She has done commercials for a soft-drink company, a Japanese sports-apparel firm, and Mizuno running shoes. And naturally she has advertised nail-care products and given her name to a "Flo Jo" doll for which she designs the clothing. She has given motivation speeches to IBM employees.

On February 29, 1989, Florence announced her retirement from track. She was 30. Florence said she was going to devote her time to writing, acting, and managing her lucrative business enterprises. Her athletic career has brought her more than gold medals in blue velvet cases. Florence lives with her husband in a Newport Beach, California, town house with her medals, trophies, and memories of one of America's most illustrious Olympic track-and-field careers.

Catherine Hardy

A member of the 1952 U.S. team at Helsinki, Catherine Hardy ran on the gold medal winning 400-meter relay team that set a world record of 45.9

seconds. She attended Georgia's Fort Valley State College and held three national indoor and outdoor titles when she qualified for the Olympic team.

Denean Howard, Sherri Howard, and Tina Howard

The Howard sisters set a national interscholastic record of 3:42.8 in the 1600-meter relay in 1979. Denean was one of the world's finest track performers. All three sisters qualified for the 1980 Olympics that the United States did not attend. In 1984 Sherri Howard was a member of the U.S.A.'s first-place 1600-meter relay team. In 1988, in Seoul, South Korea, Denean Howard-Hill ran on the U.S.A.'s second-place 1600-meter relay team.

Martha B. Hudson

She was speaking from the stage of Tennessee State University's auditorium to about 2,000 fellow students and dignitaries, who had come from all over the state for a huge homecoming celebration. Mayor Ben West of Nashville was there with shiny gold watches for the Olympic gold medalists, and Governor Buford Ellington had come as head of the state's welcoming committee.

It was a big occasion, and she was so small: Martha B. Hudson, 4 feet 10 inches in her stocking feet, was the tiniest athlete ever to participate in Olympic competition. She told her audience: "I doubt if ever so much depended on so little." The crowd roared on that crisp October day in 1960.

When she first came to Tennessee State from McRae, Georgia, Mae Faggs told her, "Why, you are shorter than I am. I have a name for you—'Peewee.'" It was a name that stuck.

Peewee ran the first leg on the American team that won the gold medal at Rome in the 400-meter relay. McRae, Georgia, her home, is in the southeast part of the state deep in the pine-forest region. Her father was a truck driver in a factory there that produced rosin, turpentine, and other

Tennessee State University's Martha B. Hudson finishes first in the 50-meter dash during the 1956 girls' and women's AAU Track and Field Championships at Philadelphia, Pennsylvania. AP/Wide World photo.

pine products. Her mother was a housewife who took care of a family of three children. Martha was the oldest.

Like Mae Faggs, Martha was a tomboy who liked to run against boys, beating them often. She went to Twin City High School where she played basketball, a game for tall girls. Again, she didn't let her height become an obstacle. She played guard and was so good that she was elected team captain. She was good at running too and had her first competition at the Tuskegee Relays.

Coach Temple, who watched her performance from the stands, invited her to come to Tennessee State as one of the first group of high school girls he brought together for a month's summer training in 1955.

A year before, the girls from Tennessee State had won the 800-yard AAU medley relay at Harrisburg, Pennsylvania, at the national outdoor meet. That team included Cynthia Thompson, a former member of the Jamaica Women's Olympic Team; Mae Faggs, a veteran of the U.S. women's Olympic team in 1948 and 1952; and two high school youngsters, running with the Tennessee State team—Lucinda Williams of Bloomingdale, Georgia, and Isabel Daniels of Jakin, Georgia. This was the beginning of the first real effort to build a women's track-and-field team at Tennessee State.

Tom Harris had coached women's track and field from 1947 to 1950, and Ed Temple took over in 1950. The real turning point, however, did not take place until 1955 at the national outdoor AAU meet in Ponca City, Oklahoma, where Tennessee State replaced Tuskegee as national champion. It was then that the name "Tigerbelles" became popular. This was the first of a long string of victories for Tennessee State's Tigerbelles.

Under Coach Temple the women's track-and-field team had won outdoor national championships 13 times and indoor championships 11 times. They had been contenders in every track meet, losing the few meets they lost by only a point or two.

Peewee was right. Never had so much depended upon the performance of one of the world's smallest athletes. She had run the first leg in the women's 400-meter relay at Rome against competitors from the Soviet Union, Poland, Panama, and Australia, all of whom were at least six inches taller. But the height and stride of her competitors had never mattered to Martha in the past, and she hadn't let it bother her then. Peewee's teammates were also her schoolmates from Tennessee State.

Ponca City was also the place where Martha Hudson had a chance to test her speed against the best female runners in the nation. She won the 75-yard dash in the women's division, and she ran second to Isabel Daniels in the 50-yard dash.

Martha entered Tennessee State on an athletic scholarship in 1957 and won her letter in track for the next four years. She was one of four students from her high school class of 26 to attend college. When Martha came to Tennessee State, Mae Faggs was the big name in women's track. "My big ambition," Martha said, "was to beat Mae just once, but I never did."

The United States' 400-meter relay team at the 1948 London Olympics. From left, Coach Evelyn Hall; Jean Patton, Tennessee State; Delores Dwyer, the German-American Athletic Club; Nell Jackson, Tuskegee Institute; and Janet Moreau. Courtesy United States Olympic Committee.

Sheila Ingram

Sheila Ingram won a silver medal as a member of the U.S. 1600-meter relay team at the 1976 Montreal Olympics.

Nell Jackson

Nell Jackson was the first black woman to coach a women's U.S. Olympic track and field team. A graduate of Tennessee State University, she coached the 1956 team at the Melbourne Olympics. She set a world record of 24.2 seconds in the 200-meter run in 1949 during a national track meet. She was a member of the U.S. team at the 1948 London Olympics, running in the 200 meters and the 400-meter relay.

Pam Jiles

Pam Jiles was a member of the 1976 team at the Montreal Olympics and won a silver medal for a second-place team finish in the 1600-meter relay.

Barbara Jones

In the 1960 Olympics, four women from Tennessee State University proved themselves the four fastest women on earth. In a semifinal heat against the Soviet Union, Panama, Australia, and Poland, they set a new world's record of 44.4 seconds in the 400-meter relay. In the finals, after rain had soaked the red-clay oval of the Olimpico Stadio at Rome, they won in 44.5 seconds, only one-tenth of a second off their new world record.

It is difficult to comprehend time and distance. What does 44.4 seconds mean? It means that a little girl not five feet tall was covering ground at the rate of 30 feet every second, less time than it takes to clap hands. That's covering ground.

They were called Tigerbelles, after the name Tigers used by Tennessee State's men's teams. This was a name that stuck, one that would soon become famous in women's track and field around the world.

If it were not enough that one school produced all four members of the 1960 U.S. women's relay team, it should be mentioned that running against them was another Tigerbelle, Lorraine Dunn, who had qualified as a member of Panama's relay team.

Running the second leg of the relay was Barbara Jones, one of the fastest women runners in the world. High-strung, nervous, always on edge, she began to warm up way ahead of the race. "She probably beat herself more times than any of her opponents by sheer worrying," one of her teammates said. As a 15-year-old member of Chicago's Catholic Youth Organization, Barbara had won a place on the 1952 U.S. women's Olympic team in Helsinki. She had run on the winning 400-meter relay team with Mae Faggs, and she won her first gold medal. In 1953, 1954, and 1955 she had been on the winning CYO relay teams at the AAU meet and for two years (1954, 1955) had been national indoor champion in the 100-yard dash. In 1953 and 1954 she had been national outdoor AAU champion in the 100 meters.

From a promising 15-year-old sprinter in 1952, Barbara had developed into an experienced 19-year-old national champion by 1956 and was almost

Barbara Jones of Chicago wins the 100-meter dash for America at the U.S.-Soviet dual track meet in Philadelphia on July 18, 1959. Russia's Vera Krepkina (not shown) finished second; Galina Popova, right, of the Soviet Union finished third and Wilma Rudolph, far right, finished fourth. AP/Wide World photo.

certain to win a place on the 1956 U.S. women's Olympic team. But she didn't make the team. In the Olympic trials she didn't win a race and couldn't even get a third place. Three Tigerbelles shut her out in the 100 meters, and three Tigerbelles beat her in the 200 meters. It was a catastrophe. When Barbara didn't make the 1956 Olympic team, she was heartbroken.

She turned to Mae Faggs, who had seen her through the Olympic Games at Helsinki, and Mae gave her some plain-spoken advice. "The thing for you to do is to come on down to Tennessee State and learn what training is all about." Barbara wrote to Coach Temple, and he arranged for her to get a track scholarship. She entered the school the same year as Martha Hudson.

You would have to have known Barbara to understand what starting over at Tennessee State meant to her. She had been an Olympic gold medalist at 15, a national AAU champion from the time she was 16 until she was 19. She had traveled abroad, run before large crowds, and heard the applause of thousands of people. Barbara was a "mother's girl" and always had been. When Barbara was a Brownie, her mother was den mother of the group. When Barbara became a Girl Scout, her mother became troop leader. The Jones family lived on the South Side, where young people were rather obstreperous. But not Barbara. There were no public dances. If Barbara had to dance, she could dance at home. She was a petted and pampered child.

At Tennessee State there was no pampering. Training was hard, regimented, and business-like. She soon discovered that she was not up against just one good female runner but several, like those who had outrun her in the 1956 Olympic trials. There was Wilma Rudolph, who was just beginning to come into her own, and scrappy Margaret Matthews, who would come out on the practice field and say, "I am really ready to give you a beating today," and mean it. One teammate said, "Margaret Matthews used to get Barbara Jones so rattled her teeth would chatter." What was truly remarkable was the way in which Barbara came through it all.

In 1957, as a Tigerbelle, she was 100-yard dash national AAU champion, only to have this title taken from her in 1958 by Margaret Matthews. In 1957 and 1958 she was 50-meter national AAU champion, and in 1958 she shared with teammate Isabel Daniels a 5.7 second world record in the 50-yard dash. Running like this won her a place on the U.S. women's international team which toured Europe in 1958. Once again she was on the international circuit.

Crowds always seemed to help Barbara's performance. The bigger the crowd, the better the race. Racing against Margaret Matthews was always a battle. Margaret was invincible on the home front but seemed to fold up abroad. Barbara was at her best in foreign competition. She was the first American woman ever to win a race against the Russians, the 100 meters in 1958, and she came back to Philadelphia, in 1959 to win the 100 meters again over the Russians in a dual meet.

At Tennessee State she ran on seven championship relay teams, more than any other Tigerbelle except Lucinda Williams, who ran on eight.

Running like this won her a place on the U.S. women's Olympic team. It was quite a comeback. She won a second Olympic gold medal, making her one of five American women athletes ever to win more than one gold medal.

The night before the finals at the Rome Olympics, the team had a meeting. No one had won a gold medal except Wilma Rudolph, who had won two. "If Wilma can win a gold medal, we can too," Barbara Jones said. And Wilma agreed to the promise because after all, they were Tigerbelles.

A hundred thousand fans rose in the stands as she swept across the finish line. Television cameras began to capture the moment as the girls from southeast Georgia, southside Chicago, Bloomingdale, Georgia, and Clarksville, Tennessee, heard the band play "The Star Spangled Banner" for America and for the Tigerbelles.

That night they appeared on Rome's television stations, and then they went to dinner at Bricktop's. Bricktop was a well-known black nightclub owner in Rome who catered to royalty and Europe's elite. It was an evening filled with congratulations, movie stars, and champagne.

The Tigerbelle victory in the Olympic relay at Rome only served to underscore the Tigerbelles' progress since their first championship in 1955. *Sports Illustrated* declared that Tennessee State University was "fast becoming the Notre Dame of women's track and field." And the *New York Times* wrote: "The cathedral of women's track in this country is Tennessee A&I and [Ed] Temple is its high priest."

Between 1956 and 1988, 40 Tigerbelles won places on U.S. Olympic teams. They won 13 gold medals, 6 silver medals, and 4 bronze medals in international competition. But Coach Temple is equally proud of the fact that 39 of these athletes received their undergraduate degrees; 28 earned their masters, and 6 earned Ph.D.'s.

Fame in track and field is a fleeting thing, and Coach Temple constantly reminded athletes of his dictum that "records are made to be broken." There is, however, something to track and field besides medals, records, and winning. There is spirit, tradition, and a powerful motivation to achieve that somehow captured women athletes who made the Tigerbelle team. What made a Tigerbelle was something besides the ability to run. One of the first lessons she learned was that she was "a lady first" and a "track lady second." The emphasis was on femininity, not building muscles. Tigerbelles didn't take male hormones to improve their strength as in some European countries.

The Tigerbelle tradition opposed permitting a photographer to take a picture immediately after a race. The runner had first to wipe the perspiration from her face, comb her hair, possibly put on a touch of lipstick before pictures were permitted. The Tigerbelle tradition was a sharp break with the image of women's track stars as "muscular, masculine women" associated with earlier American female athletic stars Helen Stephens and Babe Didrikson. Despite the fact that they were not abundantly endowed with money, it was often difficult to identify Tigerbelles in street clothes as track stars. They were more often mistaken for a girls' choir.

It was the little things that made the Tigerbelles so fast. They practiced the fundamentals again and again. Practice sessions were seldom more than an hour and a half, but it was 90 minutes of organized and disciplined training. Every athlete spent the time doing something constructive. They learned how to relax their wrists and hands to run loosely, effortlessly, and how to bring their arms across their bodies when running.

Two of Coach Temple's techniques that probably meant the most to the teams were the famous "Tennessee lean" and baton passing. Most runners run up and down and do not take advantage of bending their bodies at the finish line. Pat Daniels Winslow, a former pentathlon champion, was an example of an outstanding athlete who never learned the "Tennessee lean" until after she made the U.S. Tokyo Olympic team. Every Tigerbelle in the sprints practiced almost endlessly to lean toward the tape at the finish line, and it made the difference in many a race. In relays, baton passing is important. The three baton passes in a relay must be oil-smooth, and the timing has to be just right. The runners must stay in the passing zone and have absolute confidence in their teammates.

Teamwork is the highest essential in relay racing. Everything depends upon unity. Staying ahead, passing the baton without a hitch, stamina at the finish line—all require alertness, speed, and a fighting spirit.

Tigerbelle practice was year-around. In the fall the team ran cross-country over the open fields and up and down Nashville's jagged hills. This built stamina, strong runners not apt to get torn ligaments or pulled muscles at the height of an international competition. During the winter, they practiced for indoor meets, an entirely different type of running from outdoor track. And then came the AAU indoor national meets, the Mason-Dixon Games at Louisville, and occasionally representation at meets sponsored by the *Washington Evening Star.*

In the early spring they returned to the outdoor track for more practice of fundamentals, the techniques of running, jumping, and relays. During the summer program promising young high school students came for a month of training. The older Tigerbelles taught them the fundamentals of track and field. These summer programs provided the wellspring that built and continued to strengthen Tigerbelle teams. It was from these programs that stars like Wilma Rudolph, Edith McGuire, Wyomia Tyus, and others came.

Winning track meets requires generalship. In an indoor meet in 1965, Edith McGuire had qualified for the finals in the 200-yard dash. Since she had the fastest time in the trial heats, she had her choice of lanes in the finals. It is a tricky and difficult thing to run as fast as you can on boards around a curved track. You have to be aware of other runners on the boards. Coach Temple had to know ahead of time which lane would be the fastest for his runner. He had to talk with old-timers familiar with this particular track, New York City's Madison Square Garden. He made the right decision, and Edith won the race, capturing the American record in the 200-yard dash.

The Tigerbelles did not try for a team victory every time. Sometimes it was more important to qualify individual runners than to win the team trophy. In the 1964 AAU national outdoors meet in Hanford, California, for example, Tennessee State lost the meet by just one point. Only five athletes made the trip from Nashville to Hanford, and they were not entered in the relays, which they more than likely would have won. What was more important than winning the meet's trophy was that all five runners qualified for the U.S. team.

Almost from its beginning, the Tigerbelle team had been international. Cynthia Thompson, from Half Way Tree, Jamaica, had been on the Jamaican Olympic team in 1948 and 1952 before she joined Mae Faggs at Tennessee State in 1954. Two Panamanian runners, Lorraine Dunn and Marcella Daniel, were also Tigerbelles who represented their country in Olympic Games and at the Pan-American Games.

Tennessee State never had a white athlete on its track team, but Coach Temple had been much in demand at track clinics and as a coach on European and two Olympic teams. There was nothing to prevent a white runner from matriculating at Tennessee State. Other women's track teams — the Los Angeles Mercurrettes, Mayor Daley's Chicago Youth Foundation, the Frederick, Maryland, Track and Field Club, and others — had interracial teams. There is, of course, nothing special about black women as track-and-field athletes — that is, unless one recognizes that in few other sports can a poor black girl find an opportunity to compete and win worldwide recognition.

What is special about the Tigerbelles is the careful attention to track-and-field fundamentals. For in track and field more than anywhere else except perhaps popular music, race and color are irrelevant.

Jackie Joyner-Kersee

Jackie Joyner-Kersee jumped the hurdles of East St. Louis, Illinois', blind alleys of crime, poverty, and violence to win two gold medals in Seoul. After the 1988 Olympics she was acknowledged as "America's best all-around female athlete." She earned the accolade by winning the most grueling contest in women's track and field, the seven-event heptathlon, and a second Olympic gold medal in the individual long jump.

The long road from East St. Louis to Seoul was pocked with difficult and treacherous byways. Jacqueline Joyner was born March 3, 1962, in the same frame bungalow where her father was born, 1433 Piggott Avenue. Her grandmother named her Jacqueline, after then first lady Jacqueline Kennedy. She predicted that "Someday this girl will be the first lady of something." But before her grandmother's prophecy was fulfilled, Jackie had to conquer the barriers that stood between the dark mean streets of her childhood environment and her bright athletic future.

Jackie's mother, Mary Joyner, didn't want her four children—Jackie, Alfred, Angela, and Deborah—to become victims of their ghetto, a pocket of crime, substance abuse, and violent death. When Jackie was 10, her dance instructor was murdered. At the age of 11, she saw a man shot to death near her house. When she was 14, her grandfather killed his wife in a drunken rage with a 12-gauge shotgun. These ghastly sights and memories left an indelible impression on the mind of the young girl.

In the 1960s, East St. Louis—across the river from St. Louis—was a depressed industrial town. Most of its factories were idle. Many of its houses and stores were vacant and boarded up. It had one of America's highest unemployment rates and lowest per capita incomes in addition to the crime and violence that stalked its streets. Numerous young people about Jackie's age were reaching out from drab uncertainty for a bright future, only to find a package of drugs in their hands.

Jackie was one of the lucky ones.

"I never despaired," she told *Life* magazine writer Pat Jordan. "I always had something to shoot for each year. To jump just one inch farther. I never got into drinking because I saw how it destroyed my family. My father would stagger home drunk and say things he didn't mean. So I kept saying to myself, 'I've got to work hard, I've got to be successful.'"

Jackie showed athletic promise at an early age. She competed in track events at the Mayor Brown Center, housed in a geodesic dome designed by R. Buckminster Fuller, across the street from her Piggott Avenue home. "I was nine years old when I had my first track competition," she said. Her parents were not impressed with her fledgling track career and advised her to quit. But they changed their minds after Jackie started winning school contests. In the long jump she was good. She leaped more than 17 feet, a phenomenal accomplishment for a 12-year-old. She set an example for her brother Al, who was to become an Olympic gold medal champion in the triple jump.

Jackie and Al Joyner inherited their father's love for sports. He had been a high school hurdler and football player. But her mother, Jackie said,

Jackie Joyner-Kersee finishes first in the 200 meters on her way to a gold medal victory in the grueling heptathlon at the 1988 Olympics in Seoul, Korea. AP/Wide World photo.

was the "foundation" of the family. Mrs. Joyner encouraged her children to be polite and disciplined, and to work hard in school. She instilled in them the determination to build a better life and the knowledge that the world had more to offer than what appeared available in East St. Louis.

"We were not a poor family, but a family that had a lot of loving and caring in it," Jackie remembered. "I knew that if we continued to do things right, something good was going to happen. We didn't have a lot, but we knew our mother and father were doing their very best." Mrs. Joyner was a nurse's assistant at the local hospital. Mr. Joyner was a railroad switchman at the railyards in Springfield, Illinois, 75 miles from East St. Louis. He came home only on weekends.

Jackie was as determined to succeed in the classroom as she was on Lincoln High School's poorly maintained cinder track, five miles from the school near the smokestack of the Pfizer Company's chemical plant. She was an attractive student who earned good grades despite the increasing after-school demands of her track-and-field pursuits. Though the long jump was her specialty, she became interested in the five-event pentathlon when a coach at the Brown Center advised her she would have a good chance to make a U.S. Olympic team if she participated in more events. As a member of Lincoln High School's track team, she won the first of her four National Junior Pentathlon championships. She was 14. She set a state high school record of 20 feet, 7½ inches in the long jump in her junior year.

She played high school volleyball and was a star performer on the school's basketball team. Jackie graduated from Lincoln High School in 1980 in the top 10 percent of her class of 350 students. Her athletic ability and academic achievement had not gone unnoticed. UCLA offered her basketball and track scholarships. She took the basketball scholarship and became an outstanding forward.

The summer before Jackie entered UCLA she competed in the U.S. Olympic trials, hoping to win a place on America's team to the Moscow Olympiad. Like other eager American athletes, she was disappointed when the United States boycotted the games to protest the Soviet Union's invasion of Afghanistan. She entered UCLA that fall, anxious to learn, raring to run. Jackie elected a major in history and a communications minor.

In January 1981, during her freshman year, Jackie's mother died of meningitis at the age of 38. Jackie and her brother Al had been summoned home where they found their mother in a coma near death. The doctors told them Mary Joyner was "brain dead" and would never regain consciousness. Jackie and Al made the painful decision their father could not make. They allowed the doctor to turn off the life-support system. Mrs. Joyner died two hours later.

Jackie returned to UCLA burdened with her grief but buoyed by the legacy of her mother's determination to strive for success. She soon met Bob Kersee, an assistant UCLA track coach whose mother had also died at an early age. Kersee, a lay minister in the Baptist church, comforted her and took an interest in her athletic career. She had been concentrating on basketball and the long jump, and as she had done in high school, she earned honor-roll grades.

Bob Kersee had a vision for Jackie's track-and-field future. He saw her as "this talent walking around that everyone was blind to." One afternoon he took Jackie aside and showed her the results of some mathematical calculations he had made on a yellow legal pad. His tabulations indicated that even without special training, Jackie's performances in heptathlon events was only 400 points behind America's then heptathlon champion, Jane Frederick. Jackie's raw speed and sprinting ability gave her an edge in the 200 meters, Kersee said, although "everyone could beat her in the hurdles."

The heptathlon, the female counterpart of the ten-event decathlon for men, demands strength, endurance, stamina, and versatility. On the first day of the contest there is the 100-meter hurdles, the high jump, the shot put, and the 200-meter dash. Competitors return the next day to participate in the long jump and the javelin throw. Finally they must summon all their remaining energy to run the rigorous 800-meter race. Three years earlier, the International Amateur Athletic Federation (IAAF), the governing body for track and field, had added the javelin throw and the 800 meters to the five-event pentathlon for women. Heptathlon scores are computed by a complex formula of distances and times devised by the IAAF.

Jackie agreed to train for the heptathlon even though she had serious concerns that the 800 meters, the shot put, and javelin throw would compromise her basketball and long jump efforts. Jackie worked hard, and early in 1982 Kersee told friends that he was sure Jackie would soon hold the world record in track and field's most prestigious event.

In 1983 Jackie and her brother Al Joyner, a triple-jump athlete at Arkansas State University, were named members of the U.S. team to the track-and-field World Championships in Helsinki, Finland. Jackie had been troubled by a recurring pulled muscle, and her Helsinki performance was less than expected.

Several years later, Jackie Joyner told *Track and Field* magazine: "The Helsinki meet was the first time I ever encountered an injury [a pulled hamstring muscle] that was so bad I couldn't compete. I always felt before that I could overcome any physical problem, but Helsinki was the first time I felt my legs just couldn't go anymore. That blew me away mentally because I had never experienced anything like that before."

In 1984 Jackie was physically and mentally primed to compete in the Olympics to be held in Los Angeles. Jackie and her brother Al qualified for places on the track-and-field teams. Jackie arrived in Los Angeles with an American heptathlon record of 6,520 points, made in the Olympic trials—and a leg wrapped in heavy tape. She had sustained another hamstring injury a few weeks earlier.

Based on her Olympic trial record, sportswriters predicted Jackie Joyner was going to win a heptathlon gold medal in Los Angeles. Al Joyner was expected to make a creditable showing, but there was little hope he would win a gold medal. He told a reporter that he and Jackie had a personal mission to fulfill—to demonstrate that there were "better things to come out of East St. Louis than just crime."

On the meet's opening day, Jackie's leg still bothered her despite whirlpool treatments, ice packs, and ultramassages. At the end of the first day's competition she was 20 points behind the leader. The long jump, her specialty, was to be held on the second day. She was certain her performance would put her in closer contention for first place. On her first two long jump attempts she fouled, and on her third attempt she jumped only 20 feet, ½ inch.

Jackie had retaken the lead in the heptathlon by a narrow 31 points in the javelin throw when she beat her nearest competitor by 30 feet. She knew that everything now depended on her performance in the heptathlon's final event, the 800 meters. She would have to stay within 2.13 seconds of the 800-meter time set by her closest opponent, Glynis Nunn, the 24-year-old Australian schoolteacher. But Jackie finished the 800 meters in 2:13.03, missing her required mark and the first-place gold medal by one-third of a second. Jackie had an asthmatic condition that was under medical control, and though the temperature may have caused her some discomfort, she made no excuses for taking second place and proudly displayed her silver medal.

But East St. Louis was not to be denied a piece of California's Olympic gold. Al Joyner won the triple jump with a performance of 56 feet, 7½ inches.

Jackie was determined to continue her pursuit of the heptathlon gold medal that proved so elusive at Los Angeles. In 1985 she set an American record in the long jump of 23 feet, 9 inches at the Zurich, Switzerland, track meet but still ranked third in the heptathlon behind the East German athlete Sabine Paetz and Jane Frederick, the American. Frederick and Jackie had set world and American heptathlon records in 1984, and Frederick, on the verge of retirement, publicly recognized Jackie Joyner as the rising star of the "next generation."

Bob Kersee and Jackie Joyner's coach-athlete relationship began to change. They had worked closely for four years and were spending more of their nontraining hours together. They went to dinner, to the beach, and to baseball games. Jackie described her first meeting with Bob Kersee as "athlete at first sight." Bob agreed: "I didn't see Jackie in romantic terms of being my wife," he told the *New York Times.* "I saw her as an athlete of superb ability, like I'd never seen before." His sight soon became more acute. He proposed to Jackie during the seventh-inning stretch at a Houston Astros baseball game. They were married on January 11, 1986.

Bob Kersee, eight years older than Jackie, was born in Panama of a Panamanian mother and an American father, who was a chief petty officer in the U.S. Navy. Jackie's brother Al is married to Olympic champion Florence Griffith-Joyner, and for several years Bob Kersee coached Florence and other promising athletes, including gold medal Olympian Valerie Brisco-Hooks. Sportswriters referred to the three-way relationship as a "family affair" as Jackie and Florence, coached by Kersee, continued to set track-and-field records. During the summer of 1988 Florence decided that Bob Kersee did not have the time to give her the attention she needed and that he was taking too large a percentage of her promotional income. She decided to let her husband, Al, become her coach.

Her sister-in-law Florence is known for her self-designed Day-Glo running outfits, long painted fingernails, and cover-girl hairstyles. Jackie does not have, nor does she want, Flo's flash. "When I am running, I really don't care how I look, to tell you the truth," she said. "I make sure my hair is combed, but off the field I have always had this aura about myself to dress nicely."

Jackie Joyner-Kersee renewed her determination to become the world's best heptathlon athlete. Her husband-coach told her the dream could be a reality. She wanted to beat Sabine Paetz and other European heptathlon athletes. Bob Kersee developed a new training discipline designed to prevent the pulled muscles that plagued Jackie at Helsinki and Los Angeles. He kept meticulous records of the competitive times and performances of heptathlon athletes all over the world and used the information as a coaching tool. Jackie stopped playing basketball on the UCLA team and used the extra time for track training.

There were several important track meets ahead in 1986, and the redemptive 1988 Olympics in Seoul was just two years away. She ran and turned in good performance times at meets in Pomona, California, and Gotiz, Austria, where she posted a heptathlon score of 6,841 points. But it was in July 1986, at the Goodwill Games in Moscow, that Jackie gave the world a preview of what was to happen in Seoul. The Goodwill Games had been organized by American businessman Ted Turner as an effort to repair the strained relationships between the United States and the Eastern-bloc countries that had boycotted the 1984 Los Angeles Olympics.

During the two-day meet Jackie gave her best performances in almost every event. She set an American record of 12.85 seconds in the 100-meter hurdles and a heptathlon record of 23 feet in the long jump. She ran the 200 meters in 23 seconds flat, high jumped 62 inches, and put the eight-pound shot 48 feet, 5¼ inches. By the end of the first day's competition, she was well on her way toward a world's record with 4,151 points.

On the second day she made a good long jump and threw the javelin 163 feet, 4 inches. She was well ahead of all rivals and needed a time of 2:24.64 seconds in the 800 meters to win the heptathlon and set a new world record. Jackie had become the favorite of the Russian spectators. As she walked toward her starting block for the 800 meters, the announcer said over the loudspeaker, first in Russian, then in English, "We all hope Jackie Joyner will make it." She ran the race in a fast 2:10.02 seconds, and the jubilant voice of the announcer was heard again. "It's marvelous! It's magnificent!" he said.

Jackie finished the Moscow heptathlon 500 points ahead of her nearest rival, the East German Sabila Tile. The 7,148 points she earned broke the world record by 200 points and the grip the Eastern-bloc athletes had on the heptathlon. Jackie Joyner-Kersee had become the first American woman to establish a multievent world record since Mildred "Babe" Didrikson had set a triathlon record in 1936.

Twenty-six days after the Moscow Goodwill Games Jackie went to Houston to compete in the U.S. Olympic Festival, another stepping-stone on the road to Seoul. Houston was hot. The average temperature during the meet was 100 degrees, and it bothered Jackie. "I just tried to block out all negative thoughts," she said. "I kept reading little books I have, books on faith that tell you to just keep exercising your faith and continue to believe."

The Moscow meet had not burned her out. She had lots of energy left for Houston where she set a new heptathlon record of 7,161 points, breaking her Moscow record by 13 points. She surpassed her heptathlon long jump record by three-quarters of an inch and produced outstanding performances in the hurdles, high jump, and the 200 meters. She ran the 800 meters in 2:09.69. Jackie's overall performance gave her an average heptathlon score of over 7,000 points for 1986 and placed her well ahead of all other heptathlon athletes.

She won the coveted 1986 Sullivan award, even though she was judged against athletes in better-known sports like football player Vinny Testaverde, that year's Heisman trophy winner. *Track & Field News* named her Athlete of the Year, and she won the 1986 Jesse Owens award.

Jackie spent 1987 as a year of preparation for the 1988 Olympics. She won more points than any other woman at the Mobile Track and Field indoor meet, competing successfully against specialists in individual events because the heptathlon was not a scheduled contest. Running on her home track at UCLA's Drake Stadium that spring, she set an unofficial American record of 12.6 seconds in the 100-meter hurdles at the Pepsi Invitational. It was unofficial because hand stopwatches were used to clock the race instead of the more precise and official electronic timers used in larger meets.

That August she went to the Rome world championships and won gold medals in the heptathlon and the individual long jump. *Sporting News* reported in September 1987: "Those calling her America's greatest athlete since Jim Thorpe might not be exaggerating."

The crucial Olympic trials were to be held that July in Indianapolis. It was time for Jackie to win her place on the U.S. Olympic team. It was time to get the chance to go to Seoul and avenge her narrow heptathlon defeat four years earlier.

Jackie had caught her right hand on her spikes during the long jump and gotten a nasty cut on her thumb. She was determined not to let the pulsating pain distract her in the javelin throw. She threw the spear 164 feet, 4 inches, far enough to qualify for the Olympic team. "Concentration is one of the biggest factors in athletics," she said after the event. Her long jump leap of 24 feet, 5½ inches tied the world record held by Heike Drechsler of East Germany.

She won the Olympic trial heptathlon with a world record 7,215 points despite a slow 2:20.70 seconds time in the 800 meters. Bob Kersee attributed the mediocre 800-meter performance to the 103-degree Indiana temperature and predicted his wife would clip 10 seconds off the trial time in Seoul's cool September climate and add 140 points to her Olympic heptathlon score. Jackie's performances were attracting attention all over the world. "People look at my marks and say, 'You can't go any faster,'" she told a reporter. "I don't believe that. I believe I can go faster in the hurdles, and I believe I can throw farther and jump farther."

It was now time to go to Seoul and show the world what four years of hard training and dedication had wrought. Jackie wanted the Olympic heptathlon gold medal more than anything else. Newspaper stories constantly reminded her that she had missed it by only five points in 1984, and those stories predicted that this time she would be a gold medal winner. In the years between Olympiads she had dominated the heptathlon. She was the only woman ever to exceed 7,000 points in the seven-sport event, a mark she had surpassed four times.

Jackie was just one of 9,627 athletes from 161 nations who had come to Seoul, but perhaps none of them had come with more determination to win a gold medal than this black Wonder Woman with smooth dark-brown skin who moved with grace on and off the track. Nearly 70,000 spectators crammed the stadium to watch one of the most colorful and elaborate opening ceremonies ever held for an Olympiad. Media observers estimated that nearly 3 billion television viewers in 100 countries would be watching the Olympic Games. The whole world was watching.

Jackie and her sister-in-law Florence Griffith-Joyner were followed all over Seoul by reporters and photographers who wanted to interview them and take their pictures before the games began. A *USA Today* photographer asked Jackie to pose near a Buddhist temple. When Bob Kersee heard chants emanating from the temple, the Baptist preacher in him came out. He asked the photographer to find another location. "We got this far," he said, "and I am not going to start pissing God off now."

The first day of heptathlon competition began well for Jackie. She had a personal best in the 100-meter hurdles. She started the race strongly and was almost caught by East Germany's Sabine John, but then Jackie took the lead and won the race in 12.69 seconds, two-hundredths of a second and four heptathlon points better than her trial performance.

But then came the high jump and the pain. It was that old Helsinki knee again. She needed two attempts to clear 6 feet, 1¼ inches, far off the mark of her personal best of 6 feet, 4 inches. She had strained her left patellar tendon on the first attempt and scored poorly in the event. But she made no excuses. Some observers believed her hopes for the heptathlon gold would once again be dashed. "After the first day," Bob Kersee told *Time,* "people wrote off the world record. They were people who didn't know Jackie."

She finished second in the shot put with a toss of 51 feet, 10 inches, and then lost 27 points with a disappointing time of 22.56 in the 200 meters, though she won the race. When she returned to the Olympic Village that night, she was 103 points behind the heptathlon pace she had set at the Indianapolis trials but 181 points ahead of East Germany's second-place Sabine John.

She endured several hours of cross-fiber massages on her left knee, administered by her physical therapist, Bob Forster. She slept with the tingle of a therapeutic electric current coursing through her leg. In the morning the knee was better, but there was still some pain.

In her specialty event, the long jump, she leaped once — 23 feet, 10¼ inches — establishing a heptathlon world record 1,264 points and women's Olympic long jump record. She had moved to within 11 points of her pace. But she gave most of it back in the javelin throw. For two years she had been throwing the javelin more than 160 feet. But on this important day in Seoul she could offer only an effort of 149 feet, 10 inches. It cost her 86 heptathlon points. "It was disgusting," she said. "The knee was sore, and I wasn't using the legs. I was just arming it."

Throughout the day Jackie thought about the pending climactic 800 meter race that loomed over her like the sword of Damocles. It had been her Waterloo at Los Angeles. Now, at Seoul, it could be her salvation. She thought about 1984 and Los Angeles. And she thought about a heptathlon gold medal. "So many people gave me so much support after *not* winning [in 1984], I wanted to give something back," she said. "I thought of that as I went to the line in the 800." Bob Kersee told Jackie that despite the disappointing javelin throw, if she could run the 800 meters under 2:13.67, she would have a heptathlon world record — and the Olympic gold medal. Her best 800-meter time, set six years earlier at 20, was 2:09.32. "I knew I was in 2.10 shape," she said. "And I'd always said that when the time came I would be able to do it."

Jackie exploded from the starting blocks and ran the race with skill, precision, and grace. "I wanted a 62-second pace at the 400," she said. "I wanted to run my own race." The Soviet Union's Natalya Shubenkova was leading at the 400-meter mark with a time of 62.63 seconds. Jackie was second. "With a lap to go, my stomach started to burn," she recalled. "I thought: 'Oh no, what is this? Block it out, block it out. If your legs aren't burning you can still run.'" Three East Germans — Sabine John, Anke Behmer, and Inez Schulz — began to pull away on the final backstretch. "With 200 to go, I felt strong," Jackie said. "I even got impatient. I wanted to go on by them ... but then I thought, 'Now, Jackie, you are a long way from done.'" She went through the final turn and came down the stretch, pumping her arms in an effort to beat the clock.

Although she finished fifth, she crossed the line in 2:08.51 seconds, which gave her the points she needed to establish a world record heptathlon score of 7,291 points. Jackie had finally grasped the heptathlon gold. After winning the heptathlon, she said: "I am blessed, you just don't know, it feels good to be able to reach for something you've been striving for for a long time. ... I like the heptathlon because it shows what you are made of."

Jackie and Florence Griffith-Joyner won five-sixths of the United States' gold medals in women's track and field, and each broke a world record at the Seoul Olympiad. They appeared on the cover of *Sports Illustrated* with a headline describing them as "America's Golden Girls." They made the obligatory rounds of television talk shows and chicken-dinner banquets.

But there were a few people who wanted to discredit their performances. A Brazilian athlete had started a vicious rumor in the Olympic Village when he intimated that Jackie Joyner-Kersee and Florence Griffith-Joyner, like Canadian sprinter Ben Johnson, who was stripped of his gold medal that year, had enhanced their performances by using illegal strength-building anabolic steroids. The ugly rumor was quickly put to rest after U.S. Olympic Committee spokesman Mike Moran announced that Jackie and Flo had passed the tests for drug use, just as they had passed their Olympic competitors, with flying colors. "I don't feel that everyone in track and field is using steroids. People want to read about it, so they [the media] keep writing about it," Jackie told *Ebony*.

After the Seoul Olympiad, she brought her medals back to East St. Louis to "let the young people see those medals and show that hard work pays off." That Thanksgiving, Bob and Jackie did something else for children in her hometown. They took 100 youngsters to New York City for Macy's annual Thanksgiving Day parade. Macy's, Trans World Airlines, Marvel Comics, and McDonald's helped sponsor the trip. "There were people, when I was little, reaching into their pockets trying to make sure I could go to the Junior Olympics," Jackie said. "I feel that in return I can do that for the next generation. I probably can't do much, but at least I can inspire someone to take the right path and be successful."

Unlike earlier athletes like Wilma Rudolph and Wyomia Tyus, today's stars can participate in track and field longer because of relaxed amateur rules that allow them to accept contracts for product endorsements. This has given them the financial freedom to extend their careers. Jackie Joyner-Kersee is only one of several recent Olympic gold medal athletes to enjoy the lucrative financial fruits of product endorsements.

But endorsements do not come without burdens. Jackie had to be cautious at several track meets to make sure she quenched her thirst with 7-Up and not Coca Cola, which she was handed after one race, because she is paid to do endorsements for the 7-Up soft-drink company. She has an impressive array of commercial endorsements from 7-Up, McDonald's, Primatene Mist, Adidas, Shipman's Socks, Massengill Products, and California Eggs.

In 1992, at the age of 30, Jackie was looking ahead to the 1992 Olympiad, to be held in Barcelona, Spain, and the 1996 Olympiad scheduled for Atlanta. It seems clear that the "world's best female athlete" is still going strong. But even if she never participates in another Olympiad, Jackie Joyner-Kersee has done her part to erase some of the blemishes from East St. Louis.

Evelyn Lawler

Evelyn Lawler was a member of the U.S. team at the 1948 London Olympiad. She competed in the 60-meter hurdles and the 400-meter relay but did not win a medal. She is the mother of Olympic gold medal winner and recordholder Carl Lewis and 1984 Olympic jumper Carol Lewis.

Lillie Leatherwood

Lillie Leatherwood won a bronze medal in the 400-meter run at the 1984 Olympics. She was a member of the gold medal winning 1600-meter relay team that year.

Carol Lewis

Carol Lewis, sister of Olympic champion Carl Lewis, competed in the long jump in 1984 and finished ninth.

Mildred McDaniel

> When I won a gold medal, it was the happiest moment in my life—
> especially standing on the victory ceremony steps and they are playing the
> National Anthem for you. And even now, when I hear the National An-
> them, I think back to standing on the first-place step. . . . The Australians
> couldn't play our National Anthem too well—so we decided that if we had
> them to play it as many times as possible, by the time we left they would
> know how to play it. So between the boys' and my gold medal, by the time
> we left, they really had learned how to play it.

So Mildred McDaniel reminisced about her world's record in the
women's high jump at the Olympic Games in Melbourne, Australia, in
1956.

It started a long time before in a poor neighborhood on Linden Street
in Atlanta where Mildred McDaniel was growing up into a long-legged
gangling girl. The McDaniel family had a big backyard, and the children
in the block made a sort of playground out of it. They put two poles se-
curely in the ground and suspended a stick between them. Nobody called
it high jumping. It was just a game kids played. It was fun.

Mildred was a basketball player before she became a high jumper, but
even basketball came about by accident. One day, while a tenth-grade
student at David Howard Junior High School, she was in the gym with other
girls waiting for a physical education class to begin. To pass the time, other
girls would throw her a basketball, and Mildred would shoot the ball into
the basket. Her gym teacher arrived while this was going on and asked her
to try out for the team. But not Mildred. She didn't think she'd like it. She
changed her mind when the teacher said, "Any girl who can shoot ten
straight foul shots will get her sneakers tomorrow and will be a member of
the team." Mildred shot the ten consecutive foul shots and got her shoes.

Once on the team, she became its star player. She played with Mary
McNabb and Margaret Matthews, both of whom made the women's U.S.
Olympic track-and-field teams. Her first year on the basketball team Mary
McNabb was high point scorer; the next year, Mildred. In competition,
fans for the other team would call out "Get Skinny," and she would walk
over to the sidelines and tell her hecklers, "You call me 'Skinny' again and
I am going to shoot another goal." And she would. Soon the crowd would
begin yelling "Get Number 10." Ten was the number on her uniform.

After basketball it was track and field, but not without reluctance on
Mildred's part. This is what she said:

> It's funny how I got into track. I played basketball, and that was my
> favorite sport. And usually girls who played basketball went out for track.

After basketball season Mrs. Perkins asked me to come out for the track team. So I told her I couldn't do anything in track. So she said, "Well come out and see," and every day she would ask me when I was coming out; so I decided to go out and show her I couldn't do anything so she would be satisfied.

All the colored high schools used the same track field for practice. I went out to the track field one day, and I took a couple of laps around the track and did setting-up exercises, and then Mrs. Perkins asked me if I saw anything I would like to do. I told her "No," and she said, "Well, okay. Just sit right here for a while and maybe you will see something you can do." So I sat down.

A girl from Washington High School was high jumping, and she kept knocking the bar off the poles. So I said to myself, "She can't jump that." And Mrs. Perkins asked me, "Can you jump it?" And I said, "Sure, I can jump it." So I went over and jumped it. And she said, "That's what I am going to put you on." So that's how I started high jumping."

A few days later she said ot me, "If you can high jump, you can run hurdles." And I started hurdling. Then she told me, "If you can hurdle and high jump, you ought to be able to broad jump." And I began broad jumping. So after a while she told me, "Now that we've built up your muscles, you can be on the relay team." So I ended up high jumping, running the hurdles, broad jumping, and on the relay team."

This was Marian Armstrong-Perkins' way of handling girls—letting them discover themselves. She was never surprised or shocked by their shyness or lack of confidence. Her standards were high; somehow she made her girls feel the ability to win, and they seldom failed her.

After Howard High School Mildred went to Tuskegee Institute and to Coach Cleveland Abbott. There was strong competition at the school, especially from Janette Cantrell.

Mildred won the high jump in the national outdoor AAU meet in 1953 but lost to Janette in 1954. In 1955 and 1956 she won the high jump at both the indoor and outdoor nationals. She jumped 5 feet, 6½ inches and established herself as the outstanding woman jumper in the United States, a worthy successor to Alice Coachman, who won a gold medal in that event in the 1948 Olympics.

At the Pan-American Games in 1955 she also won the high jump title, even though she was jumping with a sore heel. Major Abbott believed Mildred would win a gold medal in the Olympic Games, but he did not live to see the victory. He died after her triumph at the Pan-American Games. Almost no one else believed she could win. Mildred had qualified for a place on the U.S. team with a jump of 5 feet, 4 inches and had jumped over 5 feet, 6½ inches. There were four girls in competition with her who had jumped 5 feet, 8 inches. Her event came on the last day and began at 8:00 A.M. They jumped until noon, took an hour for lunch, and came back to compete until 4:00 P.M.

Mildred said later:

> Each day before your event they had a prediction in the paper about
> who was going to win, and they didn't have me rated at all. Usually in the
> United States when I won, I didn't try to jump any higher, and since they
> rated you on past performance, I didn't figure in their calculations. At the
> bottom of the news story it said, "They might have a little trouble with
> Mildred McDaniel of the United States," and that's the way I wanted it.
> You see, if the girls know you can jump a certain height, they are always
> watching. So I was going to let them watch each other, and I was going
> to win the event. But my plan backfired on me because I was named first
> up to jump.

As the day wore on, the field became smaller and smaller. Several of
the 5-feet-8-inch jumpers were eliminated at 5 feet, 4 inches. Iolanda
Balas, the Romanian girl who was world record holder then, was getting
her front leg well over the bar, but her back leg was dragging. Soon she was
eliminated. Mildred had the field all to herself. But she had not broken the
world record. She was tired, and it seemed like an impossible task, but one
of the officials inflamed her. He said, in an undertone to another official,
"Well, we might as well pack up, she can't go any higher." This made her
angry, and she asked that the bar be raised to 5 feet, 9¼ inches, an inch
over the world record and more than two inches over her winning mark.
They adjusted the bar and stood back.

An announcer told the crowd of 100,000 people that Mildred
McDaniel was trying to set a new world record. A roar of applause filled
the stadium, followed by an awful silence. This was the first time Mildred
had been aware of the crowd. She missed the first jump. Then on the second
she gave her back leg such a kick that she pulled a muscle and wasn't able
to jump in the British Empire Games at Sydney. But she made that jump
and became the first American girl to set a record in this event. It remained
a world record for nearly two years and an American record until 1967.

Once the Olympic gold medal ceremonies were over—Mildred's was
the only gold medal won by an American woman at the 1956 Olympics in
Melbourne—she slipped quietly away, avoiding reporters by going out a
gate they did not expect her to use. At home, her father, a checker in an
Atlanta department store, was proud, and her mother was worried. Once,
during the competition a news boy had asked Mrs. McDaniel if Mildred
had jumped yet. "Not yet," replied the mother, "but she'll be in there
trying to jump and trying to hurt herself soon."

It was almost Christmas when she and Margaret Matthews, both from
Atlanta, got back home. The city wanted to have a "day" for the two girls,
but this was postponed so Mildred could get back to Tuskegee and her
classes. Her fiancé was waiting at Tuskegee too. Waiting also were any

number of other fellows. "When I came back from the Olympics, I had more boyfriends on campus that I knew nothing about, that I never heard of before."

The afterglow of a gold medal is short-lived. When Mildred began looking for a job teaching physical education in Pasadena, California, her interviewer was quick to inform her, "We are not interested in developing women athletes." She assured him that all she wanted to do was teach physical education. She has had a successful career as a teacher.

Edith McGuire

The fifth girl from Atlanta's David T. Howard High School to win a place on the U.S. women's Olympic team was Edith McGuire. In every Olympiad since 1952 the school had been represented; in 1952, Mary McNabb; in 1956, Mildred McDaniels and Margaret Matthews; in 1960, Anna Lois Smith. And in 1964 it was Edith McGuire. These athletes were the product of Marian Armstrong-Perkins. The first time Edith qualified for a place on a U.S. women's international team she had just turned 17 and had just finished high school. That was in 1961. Mrs. Perkins said:

> I think Edith was the most surprised person of us all when she made the team. When she realized what the trip entailed, being away from home for at least a month, she became very depressed. She began crying when she got to New York, and she cried all the way into Germany. She had a terrific homesickness and only realized that the trip was worthwhile when we got into Poland.

Running in the shadows of two-time Olympians like Wilma Rudolph and Willye B. White, Edith was not apt to gain much attention, and she didn't. The thing that kept her on balance on her first international trip was the dash. Then came the British Commonwealth Games in Kingston, Jamaica, where she equaled the 1958 record of the Australian sprinter Marlene Mathews. Then she went to the great Central Stadium of Kiev.

Here there was work to be done. Three weeks before, in Prague, Czechoslovakia, at the Resicky Memorial track-and-field meet, two Polish girls had broken the world record in the 100 meters held jointly until then by Wilma Rudolph and Wyomia Tyus. The crown of the "fastest woman on earth" had shifted from Nashville to Warsaw. The Polish girls were well known, Irena Kirszenstein and Ewa Klobukowska, two of the quartet that won the gold medal in the 400-meter relay in Tokyo. Both of them ran the 100 meters in 11.1 seconds.

Wyomia Tyus, one of the world's best sprinters during the 1960s, was seeing Russia for the second time. The first time, in 1963, the U.S. team had lost 10 out of 10 events. In 1964, at Hanford, California, there had been a partial recovery, but the defeats in Moscow still rankled. In the 100 meters Wyomia and Edith finished first and second with Tyus matching the new world record of the Polish girls. They ran away from Tatanya Talyscheva.

In the 200 meters the order was reversed, with Edith first and Wyomia, running the 200 meters for the first time, placing second. This time the two of them ran away from Vera Popova. In the 400 meters the two American champions teamed with veteran Willye B. White and a new Tennessee State University recruit, Diana Wilson of California, to win. Wyomia, running anchor, closed a five-yard gap. They did not win the meet, but they had a great deal to be thankful for.

In Warsaw they won the meet, but here there was less to be thankful for. Irena Kirszenstein won the 100 meters, the 200 meters, and the long jump, and with the help of Ewa Klobukowska, Poland also won the 400-meter relay. Wyomia was second in the 100. Edith lost to both Irena and Ewa in the 200. In that race the Polish girl set a new world record of 22.7 seconds, two-tenths of a second faster than that run by Wilma Rudolph at Corpus Christi in 1960. David Halberstam of the *New York Times* described the relay:

> Miss Tyus never got the lead. Miss Kirszenstein was several yards behind, but as she turned the corner against Diana Wilson, the American's lead disappeared.
>
> It was like a man running against a girl. Miss Klobukowska was touched about three yards ahead and though Miss Tyus was closing fast, the Poles held the lead.

There could be something to the impression Halberstam gave his readers. In the European Cup women's track-and-field competition at Kiev in September 1967, Miss Klobukowska was ruled ineligible after having failed the required sex-determination test. A subsequent *Times* story reported that "following the medical examination the doctors reported to meet officials that Miss Klobukowska had 'one chromosome too many' to qualify as a woman for athletic competition."

The Americans did not raise the biological technicality. They accepted defeat gracefully, and the Poles were jubilant. The coach of the Polish team, Andrez Piotrowski, said: "We thought we just missed at Tokyo by a step in both the 100 and the 200, and we've been waiting six months to get even."

After the Polish meet the U.S. team won the meet against West Germany in Munich handily. Wyomia and Edith were first and second in the 200 meters. Edith and Diana Wilson finished first and second, respectively, in the 200 meters. Willye White, Diana Wilson, Edith, and Wyomia won the 400-meter relay.

But for the Americans the Polish meet was an eye-opener. Who indeed was the fastest of them all? Not the Russians, not the Germans, but perhaps the Poles? The long classic stride of Irena Kirszenstein was something to behold. It reminded one of Wilma Rudolph.

McGuire went on to become the second black woman to win three medals at the same Olympiad. At the 1964 Tokyo Olympiad McGuire won a gold medal and set an Olympic record of 23 seconds in the 200-meter dash, won a silver medal in the 100-meter dash, and received a silver medal as a member of the second-place U.S. 400-meter relay team.

She retired in 1966, after a solid year during which she ran second to Wyomia Tyus in the 60-yard dash at the AAU indoor nationals and ran well at the national outdoor meet in Frederick, Maryland, placing second in the 100-yard dash and third in the 220-yard dash and sharing victory as a member of the 440-yard relay team.

Mary McNabb

Mary McNabb competed in the 100- and 200-meter dashes at the 1952 Olympics without winning a medal. A high school classmate of Mildred McDaniel, she was the first in a succession of star track and field athletes that would represent Atlanta's David T. Howard High School in four consecutive Olympiads, though her hometown was Enterprise, Alabama. She held several national records in the 100 meters and the 200 meters.

Madeline Manning

Madeline Manning, a distance runner, became the first American woman to win a gold medal in the 800-meter run when she won a gold medal at the 1968 Mexico City Olympiad. She set an Olympic record in that event of 2:00.9. A graduate of Tennessee State University, she

Madeline Manning, of Cleveland, Ohio, wins the 800-meter run in the record time of 2:00.9 at the 1968 Olympics in Mexico City, Mexico. Manning finished 15 meters ahead of silver medalist Ilona Silai of Rumania. AP/Wide World photo.

represented the United States in three Olympiads: 1968, 1972, and 1976. She won a silver medal at the 1972 Olympiad as a member of the second-place 1600-meter relay. She ran (without placing) in the 800 meters in 1976 and was ready for Moscow in 1980 when the U.S. boycott was announced. She is an ordained minister.

Teresa Manuel

Teresa Manuel was a member of the U.S. team at the 1948 Olympics. She ran the 80-meter hurdles and competed in the javelin throw, but won no medals.

Margaret Matthews

The first American girl to broad jump over 20 feet in national competition grew up in Atlanta on Butler Street, between Baker and Harris, just about the poorest, roughest slum block in the city. The slums have now been torn down, and the neighborhood they spawned has been erased, but when it did exist, it had more than its share of poverty, ignorance, and juvenile delinquency.

The girl was Margaret Matthews. She was probably the only girl who lived on the block ever to finish high school, certainly the only one to finish college. Most of the time her family lived on the $26 a week her mother earned in a laundry. Her father was sickly and worked as a low-paid construction worker a few days a month when it didn't rain. Neither parent went beyond the third grade in school. During her four years in college, Margaret did not receive a dollar from home. Her pocket money came from ironing, washing, and babysitting for families who lived near the college campus. Her room, board, and tuition were provided by an athletic scholarship from Tennessee State.

Margaret had one sister and one brother. Neither finished high school. The sister followed her mother into the laundry, and the brother, like his father, became a day laborer in construction. There was a special influence in Margaret's life, and her name was Marion Armstrong-Perkins (Morgan), a gym teacher at Atlanta's David T. Howard High School. Mrs. Morgan had a long record of inspiring successful athletes. From her black high school came outstanding girl athletes for more than two decades, including these members of U.S. Olympic teams: Mary McNabb in 1952; Mildred McDaniels, gold medalist in 1956; Anna Lois Smith in 1960; and Edith McGuire, gold and double silver medalist in 1964.

Mrs. Morgan was a special influence indeed, but Margaret explained why better than anyone else:

> I was under Mrs. Morgan in elementary school, junior high school— almost my entire school life. She did a little more than just teach me from a book; she taught me how to live with other people and for myself.

> I always wanted to do more than I saw my family was able to do. No
> one was an athlete in my family, but I saw in athletics a chance to be
> something. I saw Mary McNabb and Mildred McDaniels win medals,
> and I felt if they could, I could.
>
> I found out you don't have to be pretty to be recognized, to be known,
> to be somebody. Some people are partial; some people like pretty people,
> attractive people. Others, if you have the talent, it doesn't matter; and that's
> how it was with Mrs. Morgan. She was never partial; she always gave us an
> equal chance and I think that's what gave me the incentive to really want
> to be somebody. I carry her picture around in my wallet every day.

If Margaret had any other teacher, it was her neighborhood. At 11 she
was always running up and down the street, barefoot and full of energy,
always busy. She learned to live by the laws of her block; all the time she
was fighting, biting, and scratching other boys and girls, "anybody that
wanted to fight."

You had to assert yourself to win and survive on the mean streets of
her Atlanta neighborhood: Never let the enemy know how frightened you
really were. And this background carried over to her later athletic career
and made her probably the best brainwasher on the Tennessee State track
team.

After high school, Margaret went to Bethune Cookman College in
Florida. She didn't like it, so she went to Chicago where she ran for the
CYO. She was not happy in Chicago either. Finally she went to Tennessee
State. There she roomed with Mae Faggs, who gave her new confidence
and drive. If Mae had a comfortable shoulder on which her teammates
could cry, Margaret had a sharp and rasping tongue which kept the team
at its competitive best. "Margaret could talk a hole in your head," said Jo
Ann Terry.

Willye White, who had won a silver medal for broad-jumping in the
1956 Olympiad at Melbourne, said "I didn't want to beat but one person,
and that was Margaret." And Shirley Crowder, the hurdler, said, "Margaret
was unpredictable. I've seen her come out on the practice track and whip
everyone on the field; then we would go off to a big meet and everyone
would beat her." It is likely Margaret had made them mad enough to be
determined to beat her at all costs or that Margaret, in poor condition, had
been trying to destroy their confidence and build her own. Always she
would recall the strategy for victory she had learned in Atlanta.

Margaret's tactics could hardly have been called "pretty." Barbara
Jones, her teammate on the Chicago Comets and later on the Tennessee
State team, was a special target. This is how Margaret described one incident: "I just like to do things better than other people. I remember one time
about three weeks before the national AAU meet when Barbara's mother
came on campus. No one had ever beaten her in front of her mother, not

ever; and I wore her out that day. Every time we ran, I beat her." There is a deep significance in this incident. Margaret knew the close relationship between Barbara and her mother. Margaret had no mother financially able to make the trip to see her run; she was a spoiler. There was worse to come:

> I can remember one time we were in a national meet. I did a very bad thing and I often think about it now. It was with Barbara. I knew I had to beat her and we were on the starting line in lanes next to each other. They always announced over the loudspeaker who was going to run. So I said, "Barbara, that was your mother that was sick?" And she jumps up off the starting blocks and the starter said, "Everybody come up." She said, "My mother?" and I said, "I think so." I was trying to get her emotionally upset so that I could win. I believe she was crying as she won the race.

Margaret barely missed the Achilles heel.

There is probably much truth in Willye White's declaration that "the only time Margaret would jump was when I would jump. She was determined to beat me." It is true, as well, that out of the private war between these two broad jumpers there emerged a constantly improving American record.

In the Olympic trials of 1956, Margaret set a new American record of 19 feet, 9½ inches. Willye placed second, less than 6 inches behind, and won a place on the Olympic team as well.

Margaret was considered the United States' best chance for a medal in the broad jump. She had the experience and the best record of past performance. But she did not even qualify. The magnitude of the Olympics was too great for her. She became too tense. Twice she fouled out at the takeoff board, and on the third try she was so fearful of fouling a third time that she jumped from behind the takeoff board for a leap of only 16 feet, ½ inch, a full 3 feet less than her record jump in the Olympic trials earlier that year and far below the distance required to qualify.

Margaret redeemed herself by winning a bronze medal as a member of the U.S. 400-meter relay team, but Willye's silver medal shone brighter, and Margaret was not one to leave those who had defeated her unchallenged. She would catch them on the track and say, "You got me that time, but watch out, I am going to beat you next time." She usually did.

Having returned to Tennessee State after Melbourne, Margaret won the broad jump title in the women's division of the national outdoor AAU meet in 1957. But the victory was not a decisive one. Margaret's jump was only 19 feet, 5½ inches, half a foot short of Willye's American record. Willye was still reigning broad jump champion.

In 1958 Margaret became the first American woman to jump over 20 feet. Actually her jump of 19 feet, 4 inches in Philadelphia in 1956 had been the first time an American-born woman had jumped farther than 19 feet. It equaled the 1939 record of Stella Walsh, the Polish athlete who became a naturalized American citizen and was later discovered to have been a man competing as a woman.

But in 1958 Margaret leaped a barrier that had withstood the best efforts of American women athletes for more than a quarter of a century of broad jump competition. The event occurred in Morristown, New Jersey, July 6, 1958, at the outdoor AAU national meet. Anna Lois Smith had just completed a jump of 19 feet, 2 inches, which exceeded an earlier one by Margaret. This worried Margaret. She was always tense under competition, emotionally keyed up; a demon worked inside her when faced with the possibility of defeat. Sometimes it produced so much tension that she would crack under the strain, become unable to perform at her best. At other times it drove her to accomplish the almost impossible. She took her second jump; it was 20 feet, 1 inch, a new American record. More importantly for her personally, it put her ahead of Willye White.

And then she beat another arch rival, Barbara Jones, in the 100-meter run and anchored the winning Tennessee State 400-meter relay team which set a new meet record. She qualified to represent the United States in three events in the forthcoming European tour.

When Stella Walsh set an American record of 18 feet, 9¾ inches in the broad jump in 1939, the record stood for 8 years until Walsh broke it again. This latter record stood for 17 years until Margaret broke it in 1956, only to lose it to Willye White within a few months. The 20-foot, 1-inch record lasted just days.

There was no consistency about Margaret Matthews' performance. She said, "At that time I had not learned what it meant to win for the United States, or my school, or my hometown." Although she was to participate in the first international meet with the Soviet Union, all of the political overtones of that meet were lost on her. She slacked off in training noticeably, so badly in fact that in Moscow she was scratched from the 100-meter run and placed only fourth in the broad jump behind two Russian athletes and Anna Lois Smith. She brooded. She didn't like being beaten by Smith; she didn't like being replaced by Isabel Daniels, whom she had beaten in the trial meet.

In Warsaw Willye White, who had made the team only by reason of her past performances, sailed through the air with a leap of 20 feet, 2½ inches for a new American record. What had started out in New Jersey with so much brilliance had in less than three weeks come around full turn, and Margaret was now at the bottom of the heap. Something had to be done.

She did it just two days later. At the dual meet with Hungary in Budapest, she won three gold medals—in relay, in sprints, and with a record breaking jump of 20 feet, 3½ inches. Asked how she felt after the jump, Margaret said:

> Usually there was a marker which would show how well you did, but at Budapest there wasn't one. Mr. Temple was close by. He was hard to please. I just looked over at him and he seemed satisfied. I felt I had won. I jumped up, hollered, hugged Red [Willye White] and started signing autographs. Mr. Temple got mad; told me to put that pencil down and get out there and jump. He said the competition wasn't over and to wait until I had finished.

For Margaret, the rest of the European tour was an anticlimax. In Athens she ran second in the 100 meters behind Barbara Jones, was second in the broad jump after Willye White. Willye jumped only 19 feet, 8½ inches. Margaret did not jump even 19 feet. She dropped out of the relay. But it didn't matter. She had been traveling and competing nearly the entire month of July. Her body was tired, and besides, she was returning to the United States as queen of American broad jumpers.

The next year, 1959, was Margaret's senior year at Tennessee State. She defended her broad jump title and was AAU All-American. In the dual meet between the United States and the Soviet Union in Philadelphia, she leaped through the rain 20 feet, 2 inches but placed only second behind the 20 feet, 3 inch jump of the Russian champion, Vera Krepkina. In the Pan-American meet, held in Chicago that year, she was beaten by Anna Lois Smith; she had laid off training for three weeks before the meet.

Margaret looked ahead. She had concentrated on athletics as a means of gaining an education. Now she could think of romance. There was a campus sweetheart, an athlete like herself, Jesse Wilburn, one of the great running backs in Tennessee State football history. They married and moved to Memphis where she took a teaching position at the Klondike Elementary School and her husband became a coach at Melrose High School.

Marriage had softened Margaret but she still tried to excel. She said: "Even now I want to be the best teacher here [the Klondike School]; I believe I am capable of being the best teacher."

LaShon Nedd

LaShon Nedd competed in the 400 meters at the 1984 Olympics in Los Angeles. She failed to make the finals.

Mildrette Netter

At Mexico City in 1968 Mildrette Netter won a gold medal as a member of the U.S.A.'s first-place 1600-meter relay team, which set an Olympic and world record of 42.8 seconds.

Pamela Page

Pamela Page, a hurdler, was a member of the 1984 Olympic team. She ran in the 100-meter hurdles without success.

Audrey Mickey Patterson

Audrey Patterson was one of nine black female athletes to represent the United States at the London Olympics in 1948. During that Olympiad she won a bronze medal for a third-place finish in the 200-meter dash. It was the first Olympic medal won by a black American woman.

Jean Patton

Jean Patton competed in the 1948 London Olympics as a member of the unsuccessful U.S. 400-meter relay team.

Tidye Pickett

Tidye Pickett qualified with Louise Stokes to become one of the first two black women to make a U.S. Olympic team. Pickett and Stokes were not allowed to run on the U.S. relay team despite having posted the best qualifying times at the 1932 Olympics in Los Angeles, California. Four years later, at the Berlin Olympics, she participated in the hurdles but was disqualified when she struck a hurdle in the final race.

Emma Reed

Emma Reed, a high jumper from Redwood, Mississippi, was a member of the U.S.A.'s 1948 team at the London Olympics. Reed qualified for the team in the long jump as well, despite having never competed in the event.

Mattiline Render

Mattiline Render was a member of the U.S.A.'s fourth-place 400-meter relay team at the 1972 Munich Olympiad.

Bernice Robinson

Bernice Robinson competed in the 60-meter hurdles in the 1948 Olympics. She was a student at Chicago State Teacher's College.

Neomia Rodgers

Richard Thompson, in *Race and Sports,* describing the Executive Committee of the International Olympic Committee in Rome in 1960, tells us that it consisted of a Chicago millionaire, a New Zealand knight, a West German baron, and an English marquess. He would have had to write a different story if he had been describing American participants in the Rome Olympiad.

They were the sons and daughters of porters, janitors, domestics, athletes without money—Wilma Rudolph, Earlene Brown, Cassius Clay, and many others. And there was the representative of the United States in the women's high jump, Neomia Rodgers, daughter of a one-legged sharecropper from Roba, Alabama.

Neomia lived far down a dirt road in a three-room cabin with her mother, father and 10 other Rodgers children, five boys and five girls. She was the only one who finished the 12th grade in Macon County Training School; two others went as far as 10th grade. The others went to work on nearby farms and in the cotton fields at an early age.

It wasn't that Mr. Rodgers hadn't tried to make it. He had followed the road of tens of thousands of black migrants and gone to Chicago to work in a steel mill where he broke his leg. He had tried his luck as an orange picker in Florida, but there he fell out of a tree and had to be operated on four times. These leg injuries drove him back to the Calloway plantation. When Neomia was 5 or 6 her father was in a truck accident and was hurt so badly that his leg had to be amputated above the knee. After that he was lucky to have a place on the Calloway plantation on which he could grow 20 acres of cotton, corn, and vegetables, and raise pigs and a cow. There was always enough food.

At one time or another the family owned a secondhand car or truck. Once they even had a tractor, but the father could not keep up the payments, so it had to go back. If he was to keep his farm, the one-legged sharecropper needed the help of his wife and children in the fields. Neomia and the other children would get out of school around 3:00 P.M. and pick and hoe cotton until dark.

Life on the farm made Neomia athletic. Her physical education teacher, Miss Mildred White, soon discovered her natural ability and persuaded her family to let her come to nearby Tuskegee during the summer where she had a small room in Miss White's home. She trained with Tuskegee's track-and-field team.

Her first AAU national meet came in 1959. She tied for the championship with two girls from Chicago. She went on to the meets in 1959 but did nothing to distinguish herself. At the Olympic trials in Abilene, Texas, however, she tied with Barbara Brown of the New York Police Athletic League for a place on the team. She was 18.

She was the first member of her family ever to see New York, to fly on a plane, to see Rome. But after all, she was probably the first black sharecropper's daughter ever to be seen by the Romans. Her seatmate on the flight to Rome and her roommate in the Olympic Village was Ernestine Pollard, a Chicago girl who had run with the Youth Foundation. They trained three times a day, and when not training they went to the Vatican, the Coliseum, Trevi Fountain, and other Roman landmarks.

On the streets of Rome their Olympic uniforms gave them away, and they were beseiged by autograph seekers wherever they went. Back in the Olympic Village they listened to records, danced with athletes like Ray Norton, the runner, Eddie Machen, the coming young boxer, and they watched the young Cassius Clay eat and say that he was going to be the greatest fighter in the world. In the summer heat of a warm Italian sun, it was an experience never to be forgotten.

Neomia did not do well at the Olympics. She was the only American to make the finals in the high jump, and this classed her among the best women high jumpers in the world. But she was up against veterans, girls like Iolanda Balas of Romania, world record holder who had been beaten by Mildred McDaniel in Melbourne. She made the best jump of her life and finished 14th. She was 5 inches below the 6 feet, ¼ inch jumped by Balas.

Now the Cinderella dream was over, and she had to get back to Tuskegee. She flew all the way back, stopping in New York only long enough to change planes. In her bag were mementos of Rome, inexpensive knick-knacks for her mother and brothers and sisters in Roba, Alabama.

It was a big day at Macon County Training School. There was a Neomia Rodgers Day. People made speeches and asked her hundreds of questions. Back on the Calloway plantation there were more questions from plantation owner Calloway and his son. How did she like Rome? What place did she get? Would she like to live in Rome? Was it better than Alabama? Half-unbelieving questions from a man who found it hard to visualize his sharecropper's daughter 6,000 miles away representing the Untited States of America.

The Rome trip ended Neomia's career as a track-and-field star. Nell Jackson, coach at Tuskegee, tried to keep her active, but to no avail. She began to have headaches. School was over, and she was desperately trying to get a beautician's license. She needed money for this, and she had to work to get it. The syndrome of abject poverty took its toll. Finally her father heard that women could make good money for factory work in Waterbury, Connecticut. A woman neighbor who had gone there to work had returned to Roba with the news.

Thus encouraged, Mr. Rodgers sent his two oldest daughters, Neomia and Jean, off to Waterbury to find work. Neomia not only found work; she found a husband, a young Alabamian she met for the first time in Connecticut, Willie Foote.

Her picture appeared in the Waterbury newspaper as mother of the first baby born in Waterbury Hospital on its 75th anniversary. She named him Willie LeVoughn Foote, Willie after his father and LeVoughn because she thought he should have an important-sounding middle name.

Wilma Rudolph

Count the miracles on the road to fame. If ever there was a child with little or no early promise of athletic success, Wilma Rudolph was that child. She was born two months prematurely on June 23, 1940, in the small country town of Bethlehem, Tennessee. At birth she weighed a scant 4.5 pounds, a full pound short of normal birth weight.

Tennessee State University's Wilma Rudolph wins the semifinal heat of the 100-meter dash at the 1960 Rome Olympics. AP/Wide World photo.

Shortly after her birth her family moved to Clarksville where they lived in a rented red frame house at 644 Kellogg Street. It was a ramshackle old house that the wind blew through as if it were a sieve. At the age of 4, Wilma not only could not run; she couldn't even walk. She had double pneumonia followed by an attack of scarlet fever which settled in her feet.

She would drag herself along on the edges of her feet because putting full weight on her soles was too painful to endure. Once a week—for two tiresome years—her mother carried her into Nashville on the backseat of a Greyhound bus to Meharry Medical College, a 90-mile round-trip ride. There she was treated by a doctor who had her wear heavy cumbersome, orthopedic shoes and a brace on her left leg.

Between visits to the doctor there were long periods of leg massages by Wilma's mother or any one of her army of brothers or sisters who could be pressed into service. By the age of 6 she was hopping around on one foot. At 8 she walked unaided for the first time. When she was 10, she was running and jumping and shooting a basketball into an old peach basket her brother Westley had nailed to a pole in their backyard. Even then, she gave no thought to running. Basketball was her first love. It was a natural sport for this long-legged girl now growing like a weed.

She was the 17th child in her family, with two more children to follow her; there were 11 older half brothers and sisters and seven who shared with her the same mother and father. Her father, Eddie Rudolph, was a porter in a local dry-goods store. Her mother, Blanche Rudolph, sometimes worked as a domestic. There were many mouths to feed and not much hard cash to do it with. Wilma said she did not remember when her parents' combined yearly income exceeded $2,500. When Wilma reached high school age, Mr. Rudolph was already past 60. The chances of Wilma finishing high school were slight and the probability of going to college even worse. This was especially true for black children in Clarksville. All around her, black boys and girls were dropping out of high school. The boys went to work on the nearby tobacco farms. The girls worked as domestics.

Race relations were "good" in Clarksville, but this was because black people "knew their place." Segregation was the rule in school, public facilities, and most places of public accommodation. It had been this way since the town was built in 1748—like Rome, on seven hills—at the fork of the Red River and the Cumberland.

Most black people born in Clarksville stayed there. There were, however, occasional exceptions. Roland Hayes, the gifted tenor, gave his first concert in Clarksville more than 80 years ago. Here he had earned his tuition to Fisk University, stripping from heavy stalks the black leaves known all over the United States tobacco markets as "Clarksville tobacco." Clarence Cameron White, the violinist and composer, was born in a red-brick house at First and Main streets in 1876. It is doubtful, however, that anybody in the Rudolph family had ever heard of either of them.

Bleak as her future seemed, Wilma entered Burt High School in Clarksville after graduating from Cobb Elementary School, and it was at Burt, as a skinny little 89-pound girl, that she earned the nickname Skeeter. On the basketball court she buzzed around in a state of perpetual motion, resembling nothing more clearly in the eyes of her coach, Clinton C. Gray, than a mosquito. So he called her Skeeter, and the name stuck.

Of all the apocryphal stories told of Wilma after she became a world champion none perhaps is more amusing than one told by Coach Gray. He said that once, after Wilma had fallen on a cinder track, she told him, "Coach Gray, I am never going to lose another race." "And she didn't either," he added. Like the story of George Washington and the cherry tree, this one just isn't true, or at least Wilma's prophecy, if she made it, did not turn out to be true. She lost many races.

When she was a high school sophomore, Coach Gray recommended her to Coach Ed Temple of Tennessee State University, and she went to Nashville as one of a crop of high school youngsters in Temple's summer track training program in 1955. Wilma found herself in fast company. Queen of the sprinters on the Temple team was Mae Faggs, who had already been in two Olympics, at London and Helsinki. Mae won both the 100-yard and 220-yard dashes at the National AAU outdoor meet held at Ponca City, Oklahoma, that summer. Sharing honors with her was a younger girl, Isabel Daniels, who won the senior and junior 50-yard dashes and set a girls' championship record in the 50-yard dash. Wilma was entered in the 75-yard dash, and she ran fourth behind three of her teammates—Martha Hudson, Lucinda Williams, and Jo Ann Baker. That was Wilma's introduction to national competition. Not a very promising one.

The next year, 1956, was an Olympic year. The Olympic Games were to be held in Melbourne, Australia, and Wilma, now a junior at Burt High School, went to the Olympic trials with the Tennessee State University team. She was just 15. She still had doubts about her ability, even though in practice she was showing marked improvement. She even considered giving up track. This is what she said:

> Other than Coach Temple, I owe everything also to Mae [Faggs]. She guided me around. I didn't know about anything when I first started and she was like my mother. Everything I wanted to know or wanted to do I went to Mae for it.
>
> She really helped me a lot—especially when I wanted to give up. I'd always go to Mae and she would say, "You can do it." I was running in the finals of the 200 meters and Mae was in the finals, too. I was just all to pieces, I was real nervous. Mae would always tell me, "If you can keep up with me, you are doing fine." So she said to me, "As long as you can keep up with me you are doing fine and remember this is the last race."
>
> So I said, "okay," and went back to my blocks. I think she was in the third lane and I was in the fifth or sixth. I wasn't close to her and I was used to running close to her in practice, so I was nervous about that. So I did remember the gun going off and I looked up to find her and she was a long way in front of me, so I said to myself, "I am going to try to catch

her," and I caught her and we had the same time. Afterward she teased me and said, "Skeeter, I told you to keep up with me, I didn't tell you to pass me."

This was the way she earned a place on the 1956 U.S. women's Olympic team. During the 13,000-mile flight to Melbourne, Australia, the scared 15-year-old who was going to her first Olympic Games stayed very close to the 22-year-old veteran who was going to her third.

Despite what travel agents say, riding more than 24 hours in a plane is not an unalloyed pleasure, at least not for a 15-year-old, even with stopovers in Honolulu and the Fiji Islands. The five-course meals didn't interest Wilma. Her mother said, "She never would eat anything, and when she did, it was junk—hamburgers and soda pop."

The trip was no fun, and neither was Melbourne. It was rainy, windy, and cold. There was nothing to do but train, and training was not going well for the American runners. Things happened that shook their confidence. Their star long jumper, Margaret Matthews, fouled out of her event and did not qualify for the finals. Wilma herself did not survive the trial heats in the 200 meters, and Mae Faggs made it only to the semifinals. It soon became clear that 1956 was not their year.

It belonged to a blond, blue-eyed 18-year-old girl named Betty Cuthbert, who was to win three gold medals for Australia. Between practice sessions, the Americans stayed in their hotel rooms or went to the Olympic Village canteen to watch big fat jolly Earlene Brown, a shot-putter and discus thrower, teach the Russian athletes to "rock and roll" and do the cha-cha.

A lack of confidence pervaded the entire American Olympic team. The men's coach thought the American women were keeping the male athletes up too late. He was wrong; it was the Australian women. But confidence was most lacking on the women's relay team. One of the runners had to be replaced because of a bad case of "nerves." The team which finally represented the United States was an all–Tennessee State team made up of three veterans, Margaret Matthews, Isabel Daniels, Mae Faggs, and Wilma. And while the team had not been eliminated from competition, its performance in the early trial heats had been far from good.

In any relay, mutual confidence among teammates is mandatory. Each runner has to feel sure of her teammate—that they will be at the right place at the right time; that they will have allowed for the right number of paces to receive the baton; that as they run ahead of a teammate and put their hand back to receive the 12-inch cylinder, they will not have to look back and lose a step.

Wilma was nervous again. She worried about whether she was handing off the baton while she was still in the passing lane. Mae, the veteran, worried about the performance of the whole team, and she gave them a tongue-lashing behind the stadium they would not soon forget.

But even a tongue-lashing, when it comes from someone you love, can have healing effects. Mae's tirade did some good; it got the team third place, and the way the team celebrated after the race would have made one think their prizes were gold medals instead of bronze. They came in only two-tenths of a second behind the world record breaking Australian team anchored by the dazzling Betty Cuthbert. They stood on the podium with other winners, and Skeeter got her first taste of Olympic glory.

It was almost Christmas when she returned from the Olympic Games at Melbourne, and there were weeks of schoolwork to make up. There was little time for track during the next six months. She continued playing basketball and became high scorer on the team, but she did not begin running seriously again until that summer when she again attended the summer program for girls at Tennessee State University. In August she ran at the national outdoor meet in Cleveland, Ohio. She was still in the girls' division because she was under 17. She set new AAU records in the girls' 75-yard and 100-yard dashes and ran on a record breaking 300-yard relay team with other Tennessee State girls. Her name was now in the record books.

Then for one full year, 1958, Wilma Rudolph dropped out of track. She discovered during a routine physical examination that she was pregnant. She was just 17. Wilma had been involved in a close relationship with Robert Eldridge, a high school friend she had dated for more than a year. "I was mortified," she recalled. "Pregnant? I couldn't understand it. Robert and I had just started to get involved in sex, and here I was pregnant. We were both innocent about sex, didn't know anything about birth control or about contraceptives, but neither one of us thought it would result in this."

Wilma was raised in a devout Baptist family. She embraced the faith at an early age and credited her religion with helping her conquer her childhood medical problems. She said her church's religious code made it difficult to discuss sex openly with her mother. "I couldn't ask about such things as sex, because sex was a taboo subject in the religion," she said.

Abortion was illegal in Tennessee, and it was morally out of the question for Wilma and her family. Her father was understanding. After forbidding her to see Eldridge, whom he blamed for her pregnancy, he told her, "Don't worry about anything. Don't be ashamed of anything. Everybody makes mistakes."

She had the child, a daughter, and named her Yolanda. Wilma's older sister Yvonne, who was married and lived in St. Louis, volunteered to care for the infant while Wilma returned to school and continued her athletic career. "The people I loved were sticking by me, and that alone took a lot of pressure, and pain and guilt off my shoulders," she recalled.

During the year that Wilma did not compete, other girls—Barbara Jones, who beat the Russian sprinters in the 100 meters; Earlene Brown, who won the shot put in the dual meet with the Russians; and Margaret Matthews, who became the first American woman to jump 20 feet—were making track history.

More women track stars are lost than are found in the four years between Olympics. The motivation to train, to stay in condition, is less than it might be if more public encouragement was given to young teenage athletes. In addition, 17 is that wondrous age when girls discover boys and when working out on the cinder track becomes less inviting. Every year some of the most promising young athletes become track dropouts. The miracle is not that Wilma dropped out of track competition in 1958 to have a child but that she returned to it in 1959.

When she graduated from high school in June, Coach Temple told her he would relax his rule that forbade mothers in his training program at Tennessee State, and that September she entered the school as a freshman on a full athletic scholarship. She was given a job working in the school's post office to earn her room and board. She had to study. She had to work. She had to run.

Great runners are made, not born. When Wilma first came to Tennessee State, she had almost none of the running characteristics that were to make her famous. She didn't have the long scissoring stride that made sportswriters call her a gazelle or the relaxed looseness of muscles that made her seem to float along the track. She ran straight up and down, clenching her fists and gritting her teeth. Coach Temple taught her to lean toward the tape at the finish line—the famous "Tennessee lean." She had to learn to be a gazelle. And learning came hard.

It was the rule of the Tennessee track team that athletes showed up ready to run promptly at 9:00 A.M. For every minute they were late, they had to run one lap around the track. One morning Wilma, who liked nothing better than sleep, came to practice a half hour late. Penalty? Thirty laps around the track. The next morning she showed up for practice at 8:30 A.M. This was only one of many lessons she learned at Tennessee State.

Track practice was hard, but it was fun. Every day's practice was a track meet against girls who had proved themselves among the fastest runners in the world. Mae Faggs had left Tennessee State, but Isabel Daniels, Margaret Matthews, and Barbara Jones—all veterans of the U.S. women's team to the Moscow Olympics and all holders of AAU championship titles—were still active challengers on the Tennessee team. Against such competition she learned never to look back, because in that split second she could be certain an opponent would pass her.

For Wilma, 1959 was the year she got her "second wind" in track. She won a national championship title in the 100 meters in the AAU outdoor meet. She also won a place as a sprinter on the national U.S. women's team, chosen to compete in the USSR-U.S. dual meet in Philadelphia and in the Pan-American Games in Philadelphia and in Chicago.

In the dual-meet trials she had beaten both her teammates, Barbara Jones and Lucinda Williams. But then luck deserted her. While warming up at the meet, she attempted some limbering-up exercise she had seen her close friend sprinter Ray Norton perform. But what was sauce for the gander was not sauce for the goose. The result was a badly pulled muscle, and it was Barbara Jones who repeated her 1958 victory over the Russians by beating Galina Popova. Wilma ran third. In the Pan-American Games she joined with three veterans of the Tennessee State team—Jones, Daniels, and Williams—to set a new meet record in the 400-meter relay. But it was Lucinda Williams who was the outstanding star of the games. She was a triple winner in the 100 meters, 200 meters, and the 400-meter relay, anticipating by a year the record Wilma was to establish at the Rome Olympics.

Wilma soon discovered that 1959 was a year of deepening experience, maturity, and growing track wisdom. She learned how to ward off track "accidents"—charley horses and pulled muscles—by staying in perfect condition. She became a full-fledged citizen of the Tennessee track team, no small thing when out of 10 girls on the team, everyone earned a place on the U.S. National Team for the Pan-American Games.

Indeed, for those who know the history of the ancient Olympic Games, the Tennessee team might be compared to the famous team of wrestlers from the island of Crotona. Because of hard discipline and training, all seven of the wrestlers from Crotona came in ahead of all other competitors; so it was said: "The last wrestler of Crotona was the first wrestler of the other Greeks."

Competition in AAU track-and-field meets is the testing ground for American athletes. Here national champions are crowned, records made and broken. The king of sports, like the ancient kings among primitive peoples, is permitted to live only so long as he remains unbeaten or his record remains unbroken. There are few indeed who can hope for the good fortune of Olympic champion Jesse Owens. His Olympic record in the long jump survived all assaults for 24 years, from Berlin in 1936 to Rome in 1960 when it was surpassed by Ralph Boston. Always waiting in the wings is the coming champion, growing stronger, faster, ever more confident.

This was Wilma in 1959. Then in 1960 she came into her own at the Chicago University field house in April. She won the 50 meters, the 100-yard dash, and the 220-yard dash, in each case dethroning one of her Tennessee State teammates. She ran the 100-yard dash on a curved track in the phenomenal time of 10.7 seconds, four-tenths of a second better than the record set in 1956 by teammate Isabel Daniels.

A new Wilma had been born. In the outdoor season in July at the National AAU outdoor meet in Corpus Christi, Texas, and at the Olympic trials at Abilene, Texas, she was superb. At Corpus Christi she won the 100- and 200-meter races with ease. In the 100 meters she tied the record set by teammate Barbara Jones in 1955; in the 200 meters she set a new world record of 22.9 seconds, shattering by three-tenths of a second the record set by Betty Cuthbert in 1956. She became the first American woman to hold a world record in a running event. Her record remained on the books for five years. At Abilene, she raced to easy victories in both sprints. Eleven of the 18 athletes on the American team were black, and 8 of these came from Tennessee State University.

Yet despite the promise shown in Wilma's trial races, there were few who could have predicted that she was destined to be a triple gold medalist. Although she had missed Melbourne because of a muscle injury, Barbara Jones was the team's veteran. She had won a gold medal in the relays at Helsinki in 1952. She had conquered the Russian sprinters in Moscow in 1958 and in Philadelphia in 1959. Barbara was to compete in the 100 meters with Wilma.

No less impressive were the credits of Lucinda Williams, who was to compete in the 200 meters. She too had won this event in dual meets with the Russians in 1958 and 1959 and had been a brilliant triple winner at the Pan-American Games. And she was the 1958 AAU outdoor champion of the 220-yard dash. In the Olympic trials both Barbara and Lucinda had come in second to Wilma in their events.

Races, especially sprints, are measured in tenths of a second. Sometimes barely a stride separates winner from loser in the finals. Sometimes the speed with which a runner gets off the starting blocks determines the winner. Both girls were strong, experienced, and fast; fast enough to team with Wilma and Martha Hudson to run a world breaking 400-meter relay. On form, either of them might have been picked as likely winners. Wilma was not sure of winning. She said: "I wasn't expected to win anything, but I really wanted to win something. I remember I was talking to my mother just before we left. I said 'Well, I am in three events. Maybe I can bring one medal back.'"

The test came on the red-clay oval of Rome's Staido Olimpico. Now she was running against the best women sprinters in the world. Martha Hudson was eliminated in the second round of trial heats. Barbara Jones, too tense under the strain of competition, was nosed out in the semifinals by the French runner Catherine Capdeville, although both of them ran the 100 meters in the same time, 11.7 seconds. This was two-tenths of a second slower than Barbara's best time. Betty Cuthbert, the triple winner at the

Melbourns Olympics, was also eliminated early in competition. Running in the sixth heat, Wilma finished ahead of the French champion, Capdeville, in the fastest time of any of the winners of the trial heats. *Time* magazine said: "From the moment she first sped down the track in Rome's Olympic Stadium, there was no doubt she was the fastest woman the world had ever seen."

In the second round she defeated Vera Krepinka, who had set a world's record in the distance in 1958. In the semifinals she tied Krepinka's world record, with Guiseppina Leone of Italy and Jennifer Smart of Great Britain trailing her. In the finals, with the wind slightly less than a mile over the allowable velocity of 4.7 miles per hour, she ran the fastest 100 meters ever run by a woman, beating Dorothy Hyman of Great Britain, Leone of Italy, and Maria Itkins of Russia by more than four yards. Her time was 11 seconds flat.

Wilma became the first American woman to win a gold medal since Helen Stephens in 1936.

The story was much the same in the 200-meter competition. To her major competitors in the 100 meters were added two exceptionally strong runners from Germany and Poland—Juttee Heine and Barbara Janisewzka. Lucinda Williams was eliminated in the semifinals. In her first heat, Wilma broke the Olympic record held by Australia's Cuthbert and Mildred Jackson. In the finals she again came in first, this time ahead of Jutte Heine and Dorothy Hyman.

A downpour drenched the stadium after the 200-meter finals, but minutes later, Wilma wearing a floppy straw hat with a red and black band, was at the gate to the Olympic Village signing autographs. A wedge of six Tennessee State girls rescued her from the crowd and the rain.

The 400-meter relays final came on September 8. Competition had been intense. In the semifinals the Tennessee State athletes—Martha Hudson, Barbara Jones, Lucinda Williams, and Wilma Rudolph—running as the U.S. team against the Soviet Union, Poland, and Australia, had set a new world's record. Now, in the finals, a mishap almost cost them the victory. On the pass from Lucinda (running third leg) to Wilma, the baton was bobbled, and Wilma had to stop to grasp it as Jutte Heine was flying two strides ahead. Wilma put on a furious final burst of speed to come from behind and lead Leone, Heine, and Irina Press of Russia to the tape for her third gold medal.

The Clarksville *Leaf Chronicle* called Wilma "an inspiration to the whole world." And indeed she was. Fifteen countries invited her to appear at post–Olympic meets, and American Olympic officials, anxious to capitalize on the Olympic glory Wilma had brought to the United States, quickly arranged a tour. Wilma, her three teammates on the winning relay team, and Earlene Brown, who had won a bronze medal in the shot put, were members of the touring group. They went to Frankfurt, Germany, where Wilma was given "the world's fastest bicycle for the world's fastest woman." In Athens she competed in the stadium where the modern Olympic Games began. In London, a life-size statue of her was placed in Madame Tussaud's famous wax works, sharing popularity with one of Jack the Ripper. Meanwhile, back in Nashville, Tennessee's governor Buford Ellington, who had campaigned for election as "an old-fashioned segregationist," got ready to head the state's Welcome Home Committee.

Toward the end of September the small troupe returned to America. Wilma was tired; she wanted to go home. She had left Clarksville in June and hadn't been back since. But there was still more to do. The *New York Times* on September 27, after describing her tumultuous reception in New York, said:

> Today, with her entourage of fellow athletes, public relations aides and coach, Edward Temple, Miss Rudolph will begin the second lap of a cross country victory run.
>
> The group plans to fly to Detroit, then to Chicago and finally to Nashville, stopping for plaudits, citations and rubber chicken along the way.

Even after the welcome home ceremony in Nashville, with the governor, the mayor, and President Davis of Tennessee State all delivering congratulations, Coach Temple still kept Wilma at school for two days. Her mother and father came to see her but left without taking her home. Clarksville was planning big things. In ancient times the proud city from which an Olympic victor came made a breach in its walls through which the victorious athlete could return. Clarksville did no less. It breached the walls of racial prejudice.

The mayor, William Barksdale, proclaimed October 4 Wilma Rudolph Day, and his proclamation, engraved on a silver tray, was presented to her. He met Wilma and her parents on the outskirts of Clarksville and gave her a huge bouquet of roses. In downtown Clarksville 4,000 people lined the main street for 10 blocks. Pictures of Wilma—a funny little drawing when she was 14—were in every window. The group toured Fort Campbell near the town, making a stop at the home of Sergeant Edward Crook, the 1960 middleweight Olympic gold medalist in boxing. At the reviewing stand Wilma and her party watched with Brigadier General Charles Timmins as the fort's sports parachutists of the 101st Airborne Division made a special jump in her honor.

Nearly 2,500 years before, in the ancient Olympics, there had been another triple winner, Psaumis of Camarina. They crowned him with a wreath of wild olives, and the celebrated poet, Pindar composed the following lines:

> And since the Gods have given thee fame and wealth
> Joined with the prime of earthly treasures, health;
> Enjoy the blessings they to man assign;
> Nor fondly sigh for happiness divine.

They might have been written for Wilma, but Clarksville had its own Pindar, Judge William Hudson, and he was just as eloquent. At a banquet in Wilma's honor at the National Armory, 1,100 people, black and white, sat side by side and ate together for the first time in the city's history. Judge Hudson, his eyes welling with tears, cleared his throat and said, "If I can overcome my emotions, I'll make you a little speech. Wilma has competed with the world and brought home three gold medals. If you want to get good music out of a piano, you have to play both the white keys and the black keys." Then turning to Wilma, whom he had known since she was a child, he concluded: "You had a great reception in New York, in Detroit, but this is home."

Then Wilma made her speech. Before her former teachers, classmates, parents, all bursting with pride, she gave the pledge of a victor in true Olympic tradition: "I shall always use my physical talents to the glory of God, the best interests of my nation and the honor of womanhood. I give you my humble thanks for the opportunity to serve." Wilma was home.

But she was not home for long. On Sunday, October 9, she had to be in New York for an appearance on the "Ed Sullivan Show" before a national television audience of 30 million viewers. This was only one of a hundred different appearances that were "musts" on her calendar. She had to go to Youngstown, Ohio, for the Heart Fund; to Louisville, Kentucky, for a banquet to raise money for crippled children; to a Freedom Fund Dinner in New York City for the National Association for the Advancement of Colored People; to a banquet promoting the Pigskin Review in Washington, D.C.; and to the Cotillion in Philadelphia.

Before she knew it, "Willowy Wilma" had become "Obliging Wilma," and the banquet circuit had already added 10 or more pounds to her weight. Through it all, she was still working in the school's post office, still practicing on the track, and still trying to keep up with her studies.

Her life was no longer simple. There was a personal side. She was averaging 200 letters a day and 10 marriage proposals a week; some funny, some deadly serious. Roommate Vivian Brown said: "Some girls felt that after a fellow goes out with Wilma the race is over; and they get mad."

But she was a runner, and run she must. Not only must she run, but the public expected her to win and to break records. In January 1961 she was invited to the *Los Angeles Times* Invitational Meet as the star attraction. She ran the 60-yard dash in 6.9 seconds, setting a new world record. Vivian Brown, her lady-in-waiting, ran second. Vivian had been a speedy youngster from the Cleveland Park System track team who had made her track debut at the AAU indoor meet in Chicago in April 1960. Showing real promise, she entered Tennessee State in the fall of 1960. It was now Wilma's turn to play Mae Faggs for a promising younger runner.

On February 4 Wilma repeated her victory in the 60-yard dash at the Millrose Games in New York City, this time equaling her world record. On February 17 she was back in New York for the New York Athletic Club Games. Now she beat her record of 6.9 seconds with a time of 6.8 seconds, and right behind her, as usual, was Vivian Brown. The race was run in the evening, and the next evening she was expected in Louisville, Kentucky, to open the first meet of the Mason-Dixon Games. She had a painful bruise on her hip. Worse yet, there was an airline strike, and direct flights to Louisville from New York were unavailable. With Coach Temple and Ralph Boston, another of Tennessee State's Olympic gold medalists, she flew to Atlanta and waited there in the airport for seven hours before she could get a flight to Louisville. She arrived just 45 minutes before she was scheduled to run. Then tired, bruised hip and all, she set a new indoor world record in the 70-yard dash of 7.8 seconds, beating by four-tenths of a second the 20-year-old record set by the Polish-American athlete Stella Walsh in 1941. It was her second world record in 24 hours.

In December 1960 European sportswriters had voted her Sportswoman of the Year, an honor accorded an American for the first time. Now in 1961, she was chosen Woman Athlete of the Year, by the Associated Press. That same year, she was awarded two of the highest honors an amateur athlete can receive—the Babe Didrikson Zaharias award and the James E. Sullivan Memorial trophy, awards given to the athlete who has done most for amateur sports during the year. She was the first American woman to win Italy's Christopher Columbus award as the most outstanding international athlete. There was a cornucopia of honors and many banquets.

Finally banquets proved too much, and Wilma collapsed. It happened at the national indoor meet in Columbus, Ohio, in March. In the trial heats for the 200-yard dash she had broken every record on the books, those of both Stella Walsh and Mae Faggs. Also moving forward to the finals was her roommate, Vivian Brown. Vivian won the finals by two-tenths of a second. It was the first time Wilma had lost a race in nearly two years. In the finals of the 440-yard relays, Tennessee State had been meet relay champion for seven years. But now they were beaten by a hard-driving quartet of young runners from Mayor Richard Daley's Youth Foundation in Chicago. Lacey O'Neal, their anchor runner, led Wilma to the finish line by five yards. The next stop for Wilma was the hospital. She had felt her energy sapped by a low-grade infection that was diagnosed as tonsillitis, and after an operation in a Nashville hospital, she began training for another Olympics.

There was no time for rest and relaxation. The period from April to July was as hectic as that from January to March. She was always on the go. In America, celebrities are like lemons that the public soon squeezes dry. There is always an angle. For example, in April she found herself in Washington, D.C., at a food show as the special guest of General Mills. The company paid the travel expenses for her mother, her coach, and her. She came not to run, not to cook, but just to be there.

After the public appearance was over, a Tennessee State alumnus, Bobby Logan of Fort Worth, Texas, thought it would be a good idea for Wilma to meet a new vice president named Lyndon B. Johnson. So even though it was getting close to the time of their plane's departure, off they sped to meet the vice president.

Vice President Johnson was gracious and summoned a photographer to record the historic event, and then it occurred to him that the young man in the White House also might like to meet the world's fastest woman. A telephone call was made, and the president said, yes, indeed he would. Wilma and her mother went to the White House where John F. Kennedy was in conference with French statesman Paul Reymud. She met the president and the French statesman.

During their meeting a White House photographer had moved President Kennedy's chair to get a better photograph of the president and his Oval Office visitors. When the president attempted to sit down where the chair had been, he fell. This is how Wilma remembered the incident: "Everybody ran over to help him and we were mortified. How else do you react when you see the President of the United States miss his chair and fall on his behind? The Secret Service men picked him up, and he was laughing. In fact he was laughing so hard that he got us all to laughing."

President Kennedy told Wilma, "It's really an honor to meet you and tell you what a magnificent runner you are." The young president and the young athlete chatted affably for 35 minutes. But there was another Kennedy also anxious to meet Wilma, the president's brother Edward. So it was not surprising to find about a month later a hundred or more little Boston moppets racing with Wilma across the Boston Commons as she drew the attention of thousands to the Kennedys' physical fitness program.

Appearances are deceiving. Here was a young black girl not yet 21 meeting the most prominent citizens of the nation. She was only 8 years away from her freshman year at Burt High School, less that 13 years away from the clumsy orthopedic boot she had worn on her left foot. Now everyone wanted to meet her, talk with her, warm to her poises and gracious charm. But the Rudolph family was no richer. True, the town fathers of

Clarksville had seen to it that the family moved out of the old house on Kellogg Street to a new brick house in a government housing project, but that was all.

By July it was time for the national AAU outdoor meet in Gary, Indiana. Here not only would national champions be chosen, but members of the U.S. team to compete in Europe were to be named. This time Wilma elected to compete only in the 100-yard dash and the relay. She won the dash easily, running three yards ahead of her challenger, Lacey O'Neal. In the semifinals she tied the outdoor record of her old friend Mae Faggs. She had left the 220-yard event to Vivian Brown. Vivian ran an impressive race in the semifinals but then pulled a muscle and came in third in the finals behind two promising Chicago youngsters, Lacey O'Neal and Ernestine Pollard. But coaches put Vivian on the team anyway.

There are a few people in the world who have a talent for rubbing everyone the right way. Marian Armstrong-Perkins (now Morgan), coach and chaperone of the 1961 United States National Women's Team, was one of these. She had dedicated many years of her life to training high school girls in track and field at Howard High School in Atlanta, Georgia. Mildred McDaniel, Mary McNabb, Margaret Matthews, Anna Lois Smith, Edith McGuire, all great track stars, were her girls. She knew Wilma because she had spent summers in Nashville working with Coach Temple.

Perkins was a fortunate choice to take the American girls to Europe that summer. During the first half of the year, Wilma had gotten very little rest, and Mrs. Perkins announced, before the girls left New York that Wilma was not up to her usual form and would not be expected to run too often in the hard five-meet schedule that lay ahead. But she had not taken into consideration what the crowds wanted. All Europe wanted to see Wilma run again.

The European tour was a triumphant one. In Moscow, 100,000 spectators crowded the great sports stadium to see her tie the world's record in the 100 meters beating the Russian champion, Maria Itkina. They seemed as happy as if she had been Russian.

A new relay team had been formed. Wilma and Vivian Brown were on it with two girls who had been running for Mayor Daley's Youth Foundation in Chicago, Willye B. White and Ernestine Pollard, who first gained attention when she ran in the girls' division at the national outdoor meet in 1960, winning both the 100- and 200-yard dashes. This new team set a new world record in the 400-meter relay, a tenth of a second faster than the record set in Rome.

Europe loved Wilma, but possibly nowhere with the fanaticism shown in West Germany. At Karlsruhe, an armed guard had to block off the area where the American girls were warming up. No place was safe from fans and souvenir hunters. Guards sealed off the dressing rooms. Motorcycle police escorted the team to and from the hotel. Whenever, wherever Wilma appeared, there was a roar of approval from the crowd and the repeated chant "Vil-ma! Vil-ma! Vil-ma!" Wilma frequently wore a black raincoat, and this was the only symbol the crowd needed to throw it into a frenzy. When other girls wore black raincoats, the crowd descended on them like a pack of hungry wolves.

At Karlsruhe, Wilma again won the 100 meters, followed closely by her teammate Willye White. The relay team won again. At Neckar Stadium in Stuttgart, it was decided that Wilma would not run in the 100 meters. When this was announced, the sepectators groaned. The officials huddled and met with the U.S. coaches. The decision was reversed. Wilma would run. She broke her own world record, running the 100 meters in 11.2 seconds. For this, Wilma received the top amateur athletic trophy, the coveted Sullivan Award.

But enough was enough, so in London she did not run in the 100 meters. It didn't matter, because Willye White, who had pushed Wilma to a new world record a day or so before, went on to win the race for the United States against the British. But Wilma still had to run before the crowd, so she anchored the winning relay team once again.

In Warsaw, at the new Tenth Anniversary Stadium built from the rubble of the city left behind by German soldiers, 100,000 Poles waited to see her run. She ran the 100 meters and the anchor leg on the relay, winning both races. The tour was over.

But not the crowds. At Ireland's Shannon International Airport, a humorous thing happened. Wilma and her teammate Jo Ann Terry were surrounded by fans, and the crowd mistook Jo Ann for Wilma. Wilma was no help. She denied Jo Ann's statements that she was Wilma Rudolph and mischievously kept pointing to Jo Ann. The fans wanted autographs, so for the next half hour Jo Ann was kept busy feverishly forging the name of Wilma Rudolph. The crowd and Wilma would have it no other way.

Almost imperceptibly, old faces were giving way to new faces, but you could not tell it on the basis of the track records and trophies. The Tigerbelles were still winning track meets. Mae Faggs, Cynthia Thompson, Isabel Daniels, Margaret Matthews, Barbara Jones, and Willye B. White had all left the team. New stars were in the starting blocks.

In the 100 meters and 100 yards outdoor races a Tigerbelle—Mae Faggs, Barbara Jones, Wilma Rudolph, Edith McGuire, Wyomia Tyus, in that order—had held the national championship every year since 1955. Except for 1961 and 1968, the same had been true in the 200 meters and 220 yards; Mae Faggs, Isabel Daniels, Lucinda Williams, Vivian Brown, Edith McGuire, and Wyomia Tyus.

Other runners were added to the relay team: Shirley Crowder, a hurdler and sprinter; Anna Lois Smith, a runner and broad jumper; Alfrances

Lyman, who first ran with the Chicago CYO. The Tigerbelles had become a great athletic magnet, attracting some of the very best woman athletes in the country. By 1964, the Tigerbelles had set 6 new world records, 21 American track records, and 3 Olympic records.

At the Olympic Village in Tokyo, the room shared by gold-medal winners Edith McGuire and Wyomia Tyus was called Fort Knox by their teammates, who could proudly boast that in four Olympics—Melbourne, Rome, Tokyo, and Mexico City—the Tigerbelles had won 24 medals—15 gold, 5 silver, and 4 bronze.

The *USA Official Track and Field Handbook* is the clearest proof of all-time Tigerbelle superiority. Out of 12 listed individual noteworthy performances in 1967, 10 are credited to Tigerbelles. The Tigerbelle record was burning brighter with each passing year.

At 21 Wilma was almost ready to retire. Ahead of her were teaching and marriage. The truth is, however, that there was no good reason for her to retire. Francina "Fanny" Blankers-Koen was 30 and the mother of two children when she won four Olympic gold medals in London. In 1960 and 1962 the Russian athletes were on average about six years older than the American girls who competed against them. Stella Walsh, the Polish-American athlete, had an active athletic life that lasted almost 30 years, from 1930 to 1958. Within this period she held a total of 28 national championships in the 100 meters, the 200 meters, the discus, the long jump, and the pentathlon. There is no way to know how much faster a champion Wilma Rudolph might have become if she had had the opportunity for continued training. But here is the rub. Once away from school, there was no place to train and no one to train with.

American amateur rules were strict—and strange. An athlete could not compete for money or for a prize worth more than $70. An athlete could not accept a purse of money or receive any reward for becoming or continuing as a member of an athletic team. As a representative of the United States, athletes received transportation to the site of the meet, lodging, meals, and $2 a day for everything else. And, oh yes—for some strange reason, athletes had to pay for their own passports. Despite fluctuations in the value of currency, the $2 allowance remained the same for many years. The same economic rules also applied to teams from other countries, but there are ways of bending the rules. Consider the Russians. Their team is picked early in the year and has time off—all the time it needs—to train for international competition. Tass, the Soviet news agency, announced on January 7, 1960, the list of 62 athletes chosen to compete in the Rome Olympics in September. American girls were selected at Abilene, Texas, at the end of July 1960. At best, the time an American athlete will have after she is chosen to compete is a few weeks, and often she is so bogged down with personal duties, employment, and preparing to be away from home that she can't devote all of even this short period to training.

In 1962 Wilma was still riding the crests of her Olympic victories, but there were new names in contention, or soon to make their appearances on the track. Despite her long string of world records, there were challengers in the making. Vivian Brown had beaten Wilma once in 1961, and another teammate, Jean Holmes, had beaten her in the 60-yard dash in 1962. In 1963, Marilyn White, a young Los Angeles runner, beat Wilma in a race at the *Los Angeles Times* Invitational Meet, equaling the record Wilma had made two years earlier. For a brief period the young Californian enjoyed the limelight as "the girl who beat Wilma Rudolph."

Wilma knew it was now time to make decisions about her future. She spoke with Coach Temple about training for the 1964 Olympics. Could she endure two more years of training and trial meets? Coach Temple had told her, "You lose in 1964, and that's what people will remember, not the three golds in 1960."

Wilma decided to participate in one more AAU meet. In the 1962 national AAU outdoor meet in Los Angeles she won the 100-yard and 100-meter titles for the fourth straight year, and she ran anchor for the last time on Tennessee State's winning relay team with Vivian Brown and two newcomers, Edith McGuire and Wyomia Tyus. She qualified for the dual meet with the Soviet Union to take first place at Stanford University in Palo Alto, California. In this meet everything was much the same. She won the 100 meters over her friendly rival, Maria Itkins, and she ran a magnificent "come from behind" anchor leg in the relay to overtake Tatanya Schelkanove in the 400-meter relay.

After the race, Wilma received a standing ovation and said as the cheers were ringing in her ears that she "knew what time it was. . . . Time to retire with a sweet taste." Wilma was sitting on a bench removing her track shoes when she was approached by a young admirer. The boy asked for Wilma's autograph. She took his pen, signed the bottom of her shoes, and gave them to him. Wilma Rudolph had run her last race. But the gold medal glory she had won would continue to shine for America.

Pitirim Sorokin once observed that the history of human knowledge is a cemetery filled with wrong observations. Who is wise enough to give the precise this or that in the hearts of two people which brings them together and then pulls them apart? All we can say for a fact is that Wilma Rudolph's first marriage was a brief one and that it ended quickly in divorce. Within a year, on July 20, 1963, she had married again, this time to Robert Eldridge, her old high school classmate. But between her divorce and second marriage there came an amazing trip to Africa as the United States' representative to the African Friendship Games in Dakar, Senegal, in April 1963.

Wilbert C. Petty, cultural affairs officer at the American Embassy in Dakar, wrote of Wilma's African trip:

> I do not know of all the various parts of the world that Wilma must have traveled since 1960, but I rather suspect that this was her first time in an area where black rather than white is the color that counts. She seemed delighted to be among "the folks." She was struck by the handsome beauty of the Sengalese people—their flawless ebony skin, their excellent posture, the enviable grace with which the women wear their flowing *boubous*—a thin, chiffon-like overgarment which they drape rakishly off the shoulder. She was intrigued by the everyday life of the people, and one afternoon played "hooky" from a full round of sightseeing to spend it quietly with the family of her faithful student guide. A shy, but bright lad, he introduced Wilma to his large family, showed her all the rooms in the house and answered all kinds of questions she posed concerning the routine of their daily life. She retells this adventure with such nostalgia that I suspect it was among the fondest recollections of the Senegal visit.

Before long, Wilma was sporting a long, flowing *boubou* over a pair of gray sneakers. As she explained it:

> I really enjoyed Africa. There is something about the people that makes you fall in love with them. I just felt at home. They were very nice to me and I had a chance to be natural. I went everywhere. I even went to a place they called the "Medina"; it's a slum area. I just went out like I belonged there. They accepted me and that's what I wanted them to do. And whatever they wore, I wore. They wore short pants and tennis shoes; I wore short pants and tennis shoes. Sometimes they went without shoes; I went without mine. The women have a hairstyle. They wear a bandana around their heads, so I wore one around mine.

But all of the trip was not as informal and easygoing. Now she was in the hands of American diplomats eager to exploit the magical presence of *La Gazelle Noire* in French West Africa. She had come to Africa straight from a hospital where she had undergone minor surgery, but from the moment she stepped off the plane at Dakar's Yoff International Airport, she was on parade. Some 5,000 publicity pictures of Wilma had been distributed by the U.S. embassy all over Dakar, and at least a thousand Dakarois presented the photographs to her to be autographed. She had to make presentations on radio and appear on television, meet the international press, pay her respects to President Leopold Senghor of Senegal, give out gold medals to the winners at Friendship Stadium while 15,000 spectators cheered her wildly.

And she had to answer questions about racial segregation in the United States asked by students at the University of Dakar. She appeared at the premier performance of a U.S. Information Service film on her life entitled *Wilma Rudolph, Championne Olympique*; met with dozens of youth groups; paid courtesy calls on Ousmane N'Gom, mayor of the city of Thies and first vice president of the National Assembly, and Maurice Herzog, French minister of youth and sports, who gave her a bouquet of roses and thanked her for the tremendous prestige her presence added to the games. And then she had to appear with the teams of each of the 28 African nations competing in the games.

When it was all over, a French embassy official told a member of the American embassy, enviously, that America had won more prestige from the thousand or so dollars spent for Wilma Rudolph's travel expenses than France gained after paying the $4 million the games reportedly cost.

After the Friendship Games there was more travel in Africa for Wilma as "Ambassadress of American Sports." She went to Accra, Ghana; Conakry, Guinea; Bamako, Mali; and Ouagadougou, Upper Volta. Wherever she went, her youth, naturalness and boundless good humor won her new friends by the thousands. Young people, athletes, American embassy officials, and African diplomats greeted her at airports. Always there were school assemblies to meet students and eager young athletes anxious to have Wilma teach them to run. In suburban Donka, outside Conakry, students of the secretarial school greeted her with singing and folk dancing. Before long, Wilma was in the group, dancing with all the rest. At the National Lycée in Ouagadougou, surrounded by some 600 students under a broiling sun, she showed the track team how to use starting blocks. "Don't worry if you fall on your face a few times until you get used to the stance," she told them. "I did it myself in the beginning."

Her African friends plied her with gifts. Guinean students gave her a rare collection of records of Guinean music. Upper Voltan postal workers, impressed by the fact that she had worked her way through college in Tennessee State's post office, gave her a unique collection of Upper Voltan stamps. Rare gifts, warm friendships, and heaping banquet plates of African couscous and American turkey were all part of the routine of an Olympic champion in Africa.

She came back from Africa in June and was married in July. Not just the State Department but big private corporations had ideas about capitalizing on Wilma's fame. One company reportedly was ready to pay her $25,000 a year. They bargained without considering the most dominant trait in all of Wilma's personality—her strong will to be herself.

On the day she returned from her trip, Coach Gray was killed in an automobile accident. Deeply saddened, she considered canceling plans for a goodwill tour of Asia. But she went on the trip because she thought it a fitting tribute to the man who had done so much to inspire her.

Wilma said shortly after she retired from track that she wanted to help inspire young people:

> My main concern is young people and this is what I like to do. I like
> to be with them. I like to be treated, as you know, as everybody else—just
> as anybody, an ordinary person. And I like to take part in everything. I like
> to train them in all fields—any type of sports. That's what I like to do with
> young people. My main reason for staying here is to help Negro children.
> I really know what Negro children are missing, because I grew up here....
> Maybe one day I'll be able to put up something that they really need;
> something that would help them, you know, stay out of trouble.

Wilma returned to Clarksville and took a job teaching and coaching in
the public school she had attended as a child. She had received her degree
in education from Tennessee State. She left Clarksville a short time later to
direct a community center in Evansville, Indiana, then moved to Poland
Springs, Maine, to direct a community recreation center. In 1964 her son
Djuana was born, named by her brother Westley, who began picking a name
six months before the boy was born. She had resisted the lure of the "big job"
for a quite ordinary one teaching second grade and coaching basketball.

But Wilma got a real opportunity to use her skills and recognition to
help others in 1967 when Vice President Hubert Humphrey asked her to
participate in Operation Champ, a program designed to encourage sport
participation among the nation's disadvantaged young people.

With other athletes she traveled to 16 of America's largest ghettos, encouraging and inspiring young people whose horizons had been limited by
prejudice and poverty. Wilma understood what it meant to grow up black
and poor. She later wrote:

> After working in such places, you came away with mixed feelings, or at
> least the feeling that you shouldn't sit in judgment of anybody.... I grew
> up in a small, segregated southern town, but the oppression there was
> nothing compared to the oppression I saw in the big city black ghettos.

Deborah Sapenter

Deborah Sapenter ran on the 1976 team at the Montreal Olympics and
won a silver medal in the 1600-meter relay.

Anna Lois Smith

Anna Smith competed in the long jump at the 1960 Rome Olympics
but did not win a medal.

Louise Stokes

William H. Quaine, park commissioner of Malden, Massachusetts, in 1930, was looking for speedy young girls to join a track team he was forming. Someone told him that "the fastest thing in the schoolyard at Beebe Junior High School is a little colored girl named Louise." That is how Louise Stokes became a member of the Onteora Club and soon earned the nickname "The Malden Meteor." At least almost how.

Louise was the daughter of William H. Stokes, who maintained the lawns of Malden's wealthy citizens, and Mary W. Stokes, a domestic. The Stokes family lived in a brown double house at 55 Faulkner Street, and since both parents were away from home most of the day, it was Louise's lot as the oldest child to care for her younger sisters and brothers. She would pick the children up from a day nursery after she got out of school and take them home to change them from their "good clothes" into play clothes, and while they scampered about in the backyard, she would begin the family dinner. So when Louise asked her mother if she could join the Onteora Club, the answer was a limited "yes"; but she had to keep up with taking care of the children, her household chores and her schoolwork. It was quite a schedule. But it worked, and in time the Faulkner Street house was a showplace of medals and trophies won by Louise and, in time, by her younger sister Agnes.

Louise took part in the first women's indoor track meet ever held in Boston. She set a new American record in the standing broad jump and tied the world record. In September 1931, at Boston's Fenway Park, she won the Mayor James M. Curley trophy for the outstanding women's track performance of the year. She was first in the 100 meters, second in the 50 meters and third in the high jump, clearing 4 feet, 9 inches. In winning the Curley Cup she beat Mary Carew, star runner of the Medford Girls Club.

In the 1932 Olympic trials she tied with Mary Carew for fourth place in the 100 meters. The other black runner, Tidye Pickett, ran sixth, but both made the Olympic team, and it was understood that the last three runners in the 100 meters were to compete on the U.S. 400-meter relay team.

The 1932 Olympiad was in Los Angeles. The American team traveled to the games by train, stopping off for a night in Denver, Colorado, to break the trip. In Denver the team stayed in a hotel, but Louise and Tidye were told they would have to take their meals in their room because blacks were not allowed in the hotel's dining room. Louise and Tidye were distressed that the U.S. Olympic Committee would allow them to be treated as "second-class citizens." Their tensions only increased following an incident between Tidye and Mildred "Babe" Didrikson (Zaharias), who was to win two gold medals at this Olympiad.

It happened on the train from Denver to Los Angeles. In the Pullman car, Louise Stokes was in an upper berth, and Tidye Pickett was in the lower berth beneath her. The trains were slow in those days and frequently stopped for ice and other provisions. What under normal circumstances would have been passed off as just rambunctious horseplay among anxious young athletes became an ugly incident. Babe Didrikson threw a pitcher of ice water on Tidye Pickett as she lay in her berth. There were words—harsh, bitter words which didn't help the team's morale.

The end was not in sight. There was more to follow in Los Angeles. Stokes and Pickett trained every day with the rest of the team. They believed that they were training to run on the U.S. 400-meter relay team, and they were happy. But their joy was not to last. Rus Cowan, of the *Chicago Defender,* told it in this way:

> Olympic Village, California: July 26—Lily-whiteism, a thing more pronounced than anything else around here on the eve of the Olympic Games, threatened to oust Tidye Pickett and Louise Stokes from participation and put in their stead two girls who did not qualify.
>
> Tidye Pickett of Chicago and Louise Stokes of Boston are two girls who qualified at the final trials held in Evanston two weeks ago.... However, a meeting held Tuesday resulted in the officials deciding that two of the girls failing to qualify on the coast are much faster and should be placed ahead of the Race stars.

It is too late now, of course, to decide who was faster. On form, however, Louise Stokes had beaten Mary Carew in New England and had run a dead heat with her in the trials. It would have been just as easy for the officials to have given Louise Stokes the place she earned. Thirty-five years later, in retrospect, Louise, then Mrs. Louise Fraiser of West Medford, Massachusetts, said: "A pretty fast stunt was pulled. The only thing that would have helped us was to have a man stand up for us as well as going to all the meetings. This is what happened when we didn't have anyone to support us."

But although the two girls did not compete, they did have the thrill of association with thousands of athletes from all over the world. Hollywood, near Los Angeles, was the motion picture capital of the world, and many movie stars attended a lunch for the U.S. Olympic team at the Ambassador Hotel. Among the stars was Janet Gaynor, the reigning American sweetheart of the movies. With Charles Farrell she had just completed the saccharine Fox film *First Years.* She took a liking to Louise, and although the first black girl to make a U.S. Olympic team did not get a chance to run a race or win a gold medal, she did receive a tiny pink-gold compact from Janet Gaynor.

With the Los Angeles Olympic Games behind them, both Louise and

Tidye redoubled their efforts toward athletic improvement. Babe Didrikson was forgotten; she had given an unauthorized commercial endorsement for an automobile company and in the ensuing hassle with the AAU had turned professional and taken up golf.

In 1933, in the indoor nationals, Tidye ran second in the 50 meters. In the outdoor nationals, Louise beat Wilhelmina Von Bremen of San Francisco and Ethel Harrington of the Illinois AC in the 50 meters. Both had finished ahead of her at the Olympic trials the year before. She ran second in the 100 meters. In 1934, Louise ran third in the 50 meters behind the indomitable, and now questionable, Stella Walsh, and Tidye was fourth in the 50-meter hurdles. In 1935, Louise was again crowned national outdoor 50-meter champion, and in the 1936 indoor meet Tidye won first place in the 50-meter hurdles. Both athletes had made considerable progress since the 1932 Olympics.

They both competed in the Olympic trials for the 1936 Olympics. Tidye ran second in the trials for the 80-meter hurdles and made the team. Things did not go as well for Louise. The star of the Olympic trials that year was a tall, lanky, ungainly farm girl from the Missouri Ozarks, Helen Stephens. She could broad jump, shot put, throw the discus, and run. At Berlin she was to become the 100-meter champion, and she dominated the Olympic trials in the United States.

Louise did not qualify for the team at the trials, but Olympic Officials, mindful of her past performances and perhaps her unfair treatment four years earlier, made her a member of the team anyway. But it was still uncertain whether she could make the trip to Berlin because of the limited funds available to the U.S. Olympic Committee. Finally word came that she was going to Berlin. The *Chicago Defender* wrote: "A last minute flash from headquarters of the U.S. Olympic Team in New York City announced that the necessary funds for Miss Louise Stokes, Malden, Mass., had been secured and that she would join her teammates on the U.S.S. *Manhattan.* It was almost sailing time before Miss Stokes was aware that she would go along. There is no happier athlete on the boat than she."

Aboard ship, Louise and Tidye stayed together in an extra-large cabin, big enough to hold a card table, and because Tidye was seasick from the time she went on board until the ship docked in Hamburg, their room became the headquarters of the black athletes. Louise was the better sailor and each morning was on deck early, working out and keeping in condition.

Berlin was seething in 1936. Hitler was in power. But the Germans were on their good behavior as far as foreign athletes were concerned. Berlin was even better than Denver had been in 1932, for in Berlin a huge banquet was given for all the Olympic athletes. Hitler was there, and the American team was seated near him. "I was so close to him that I could have reached out and touched his neck," said Louise.

On the streets the black athletes were a constant source of wonder to Berliners. Louise said: "They would just stare and stare and never stop looking. I have actually seen them staring so hard that an automobile has come up and hit them."

But it was a friendly curiosity. Everywhere the black athletes went in Berlin—to the Tiegarten, the famous avenue Unter den Linden, the Brandenburg Gate—there were autograph seekers. Louise said: "Tidye and I signed autographs on cuffs, shirt collars, belts, gloves and even the hem of a petticoat. Everywhere we went it was autograph, autograph, autograph."

But at trackside there was still skullduggery. Once again it was assumed that Louise would run in the 400-meter relays; she practiced every day. But once again it was decided in "meetings" that she was not to run. The first black woman ever chosen to be a member of the U.S. women's Olympic team never ran a race. Her teammate, Tidye, did compete this time, but she hit a hurdle in the semifinals and was eliminated.

For Louise, this was the end of her track career. Stella Walsh urged her to come to Cleveland and join the Polish Women's Athletic Club. Louise's mother felt she was too young to travel alone, but it was a sincere tribute from one great athlete to another.

In a country where anything less than complete victory is considered insignificant, the performance of these two black athletes was hardly noticed. The black press published their pictures in Olympic uniforms when they returned from Berlin, but the big news was Jesse Owens, who left Berlin with four gold medals. Each girl had made two Olympic teams. Each had been chosen from the best athletes in the United States.

Jo Ann Terry

For one who has done so much for women's track, Jo Ann Terry deserves better than she has received. She was twice a member of the U.S. women's Olympic team, at Rome in 1960 and at Tokyo in 1964, but most of her accomplishments went unappreciated in her hometown of Indianapolis. The *Indianapolis Star* probably never knew it, but it was responsible for her going to Tokyo. She had been entered as a candidate for the pentathlon, an event she had handily won in 1960, but she had hard luck all the way. She had hoped to score a large number of points in the hurdles, only to fall far behind. She waited to jump in the high jump until the bar was put at 5 feet. At that height she missed three times and lost points. In the shot put her performance was 10 feet short of what she had done in practice. Her performance was disappointing. This is where the *Indianapolis Star* unwittingly played a role that improved her performance. The paper had carried the snide comment that Jo Ann Terry was going to compete in the Olympic trials but that after the trials she would probably find herself "back in the kitchen." If the paper had said "back in the schoolroom," it would have been all right, for Jo Ann was a schoolteacher. So Jo Ann, determined to make a prevaricator out of the *Indianapolis Star,* entered the long jump, and there she came in third with a jump of 19 feet, 11¼ inches, enough to guarantee her a place on the U.S. women's team for a second time.

Jo Ann was also angry at the treatment she received from the governor of Indiana. In May 1963 she came back from Sao Paulo, Brazil, with a gold medal for winning the 80-meter hurdles in the fourth Pan-American Games. Every gold medalist had a telegram of congratulations waiting for him or her from the governor of his or her state, but not Jo Ann. It made her feel like a second-class citizen. And she felt no better when the local Chamber of Commerce gave a banquet for members of the Olympic swimming team but did not invite her. It was little snubs like this that made black athletes question giving their best for the United States.

Such slights laid the early foundation for unrest among black Olympic athletes and supported claims like the one by Harry Edwards, who said that "all is not well in the locker room." Predicting a black boycott of the 1968 Olympic Games, Edwards said: "It seems as though the only way we can reach a lot of people is by showing them that all is not well in the locker room. Then maybe they'll see beyond the locker room. No one attempts to change anything he's not in love with, and the Negro loves his country, fights for it in war, and runs for it. The tragedy here is that the country the Negro loves doesn't love him back." Edwards remarks were prophetic, as shown by the protest of black athletes at the 1968 Olympic Games in Mexico City.

Despite her treatment, Jo Ann was not an embittered person. She maintained her soft and sentimental side. On the 1963 European tour she was a "big sister" to the young hurdler Tammie Davis, helping her and encouraging her. Jo Ann was married the day after President John F. Kennedy, her favorite president, was assassinated in Dallas, and she spent most of her honeymoon in tears.

Jo Ann was a truly great competitor. In 1960 she won the 80-meter hurdles championship by beating Shirley Crowder. A week later she lost to Shirley in the Olympic trials for Rome. In Emporia, Kansas, that year, she won the pentathlon. From 1959 through 1962, she was national champion in the indoor 70-meter hurdles, and she set a new American record of 9.2 seconds.

Runners from the United States and Great Britain take the first hurdle in the women's 80-meter hurdles event in 1963, a dual track-and-field meet in London. From left are Anne Charlesworth of Britain, Jo Ann Terry of the United States, Pat Nutting of Britain and Rosie Bonds of the United States. Bonds won the race in 11.1 seconds. AP/Wide World photo.

She went to Rome in 1960 and Tokyo in 1964 as a member of the 400-meter relay team, but in neither Olympiad did she run in the finals.

Her best performance came after she left Tennessee State and went to Indianapolis to teach school. Unable to get regular training, she would nevertheless come back to Tennessee State and work out with the women's track team there. She continued to encourage and support the careers of rising stars who were to continue the proud tradition to which she had contributed so much.

Angela Thacher

Angela Thacher finished fourth in jump competition at the Los Angeles Olympiad in 1984.

Debbie Thompson

Not since Barbara Frietchie has anyone brought as much fame to Frederick, Maryland, as Debbie Thompson. And gray-haired Barbara may only be a legend, for there are those who testify she was 96 years old and bedridden when General Stonewall Jackson marched through the town and that she could not possibly have defied him to strike down "Old Glory." But as the *Frederick Post* proclaimed in its lead story about the 10-year-old black girl in February 1962, "Debbie Thompson is for real. No track mirage is she."

Debbie was the first citizen of Maryland of any race or sex to win a place on a U.S. Olympic track team. Her victories in the brief period she competed in national and international track meets brought track fame to her small hometown.

In 1964 Debbie went to Tokyo as a member of the U.S. Olympic team. In 1965 the U.S. State Department sent her to Australia as one of its athletic goodwill ambassadors. She then went to Europe as a member of the U.S. team competing in indoor track meets in Poland and West Germany—all of this while she was still 17.

How all of this could happen to the daughter of a shoe repairman is a paradox, and to solve the puzzle we must turn to the U.S. Supreme Court. When Chief Justice Earl Warren in 1954 handed down the Court's decision that segregation in public schools was unconstitutional and must be ended with "all deliberate speed," Debbie was 6. Frederick began desegregation of its schools with "all deliberate speed." Debbie and another small black girl, Tamara Davis, were in Frederick's first integrated class. For the next five years everything went smoothly. A white physical education teacher in Frederick's school system made a major contribution to the town's racial progress.

Jack Griffin, a native of Frederick, had been a member of New York University's track team and a star javelin thrower. He was athletic director of Frederick's elementary school, and that is where he met Debbie Thompson. One day, one of his teachers came to him and said, "I have a little girl in my class who is 11 years old and has run the 50-yard dash in 6.8 seconds." "You must have read the stopwatch wrong," replied Griffin. "Are you sure it wasn't 8.6 seconds?" The teacher said she was sure. About an hour later, another teacher reported to Griffin that she also had an 11-year-old girl who had run the 50-yard dash in 6.8 seconds. Again Griffin was incredulous, but this time he thought he would investigate. He could at least show his physical education teachers how to read a stopwatch.

That was how Debbie Thompson and Tammie Davis met Jack Griffin. The teachers needed no lessons in reading a stopwatch. The two

Debbie Thompson, of the Frederick, Maryland, Track and Field Club wins the 50-yard dash in 6 seconds flat at the Inquirer meet in Philadelphia on February 2, 1963. Germany's Jutte Heine, right, finished second. AP/Wide World photo.

11-year-olds could and did run the 50-yard dash in 6.8 seconds over and over, a phenomenal speed for girls that age.

Years later, when Debbie and Tammie had brought fame to Frederick and its track-and-field club, a local minister told Jack Griffin that it must have been the hand of God that brought Griffin and the girls together.

Frederick used to be a different kind of town. Sharp lines divided the races. Schools were segregated. Blacks were not allowed to use the public library. The *Frederick Post* would not publish the picture of a black person, let alone run a front-page story on one. Blacks were welcome only in the all-black public park. Jack Griffin tells the story of how he invited a black college student to shoot basketball goals with him in the "white" park and how within minutes a police car arrived and the black youth was ordered out of the park.

The transformation that took place in Frederick was hard to believe. Schools, libraries, and parks were soon opened to all.

There isn't any doubt that a great deal of the racial progress in Frederick

was due in part to the track accomplishments of Debbie Thompson and
Tammie Davis, as Frederick citizens proudly basked in the accomplishments of these native daughters. A track enthusiast, Bucky Summers,
sports editor of the *Frederick Post,* was in the vanguard of those who ap-
plauded the performance of the interracial Frederick Track and Field
Club and especially its two outstanding black stars, Debbie and Tammie.
The publisher of the *Post* paid for the team's suits. Before Debbie went
off to the Tokyo Olympics, an Appreciation Dinner, attended by several
hundred black and white citizens, was given in her honor. The *Post* published a front-page picture of Debbie and Tammie with Coach Griffin
and J. Harold Hooper, president of the Frederick Senior Chamber of
Commerce, who had raised $5,000 from Frederick citizens for the team's
expenses.

As Debbie said, "It seems funny that in a little town like this, the white
and colored people can get along so good, and yet they have trouble in big
cities where they have so much more."

Debbie's father had a shoe repair shop on Frederick's Main Street. In
a wry sort of way his daughter's fame spilled over on him. A man with a
name similar to his fell out of a window one day and was fatally injured.
Debbie's home was flooded with messages of condolence. Her father asked
a local radio station to correct the obvious misunderstanding. The station
announced: "The man who suffered the fatal fall last week was not the
father of Debbie Thompson."

From 1959 to 1964, Jack Griffin and Debbie and Tammie were almost
inseparable. At least five days a week for an hour or more they were working
out under his tutelage: practicing starts, arm action, hurdle techniques, and
general conditioning. They were only two of the members of a team of
about 30 girls, about half white and half black.

At first, black athletes predominated on the team. Some white parents
didn't like the idea of their daughters participating in track with black
athletes. The mother of an especially promising 11-year-old refused her
daughter permission to join the team. She was afraid of "all the fights
Negro girls have." Later, when there was a wonderful harmony and team
spirit among all of the girls on the team, she relented, but only after her
daughter had missed a critical two years of training.

Jack Griffin stuck to his task. Almost from the beginning he turned out
winning teams. They went to the Junior Olympics. Debbie Thompson won
the 50-yard dash for 12-year-olds; Tammie Davis was second. Tammie
won the standing broad jump; Debbie was second. They took state meets
at Baltimore and won the acclaim of the school community. Frederick itself
had yet to wake up. In 1961 Griffin took his team to the AAU outdoor
nationals at Gary, Indiana. Debbie and Tammie were entered in the girls'
division. In her first national competition Tammie set a new American

record in the 50-meter hurdles. Debbie, not so fortunate, ran sixth in the 50-yard dash, which was won by Edith McGuire.

During the next three years, Tammie kept lowering her record. Debbie became one of the best sprinters in the nation. When she was 14, Debbie finished second in the women's invitational indoor 60-yard dash at the AAU nationals, running less than one-twentieth of a second behind Willye B. White, whose time of 6.8 seconds equaled the world record of Wilma Rudolph. At the 1962 women's indoor national, she took second place in both the 50- and 75-yard dashes behind Wyomia Tyus and second in the women's 50- and 60-yard dashes behind the veteran Olympic sprinter Willye B. White.

Over two days of competition and a score of trial heats, semifinals, and finals, Debbie won a place in every event she entered. At the Long Island Invitational she won three gold medals and was awarded the trophy as the meet's most outstanding athlete.

As a 15-year-old, Tammie Davis made the U.S. team which competed in Europe in the summer of 1963. Youngest member of the team, she was the special friend of Olympic stars Jo Ann Terry and Ralph Boston, her big sister and big brother. She had equaled Jo Ann's world record in the 70-yard hurdles that year. Throughout the trip, Tammie was a wide-eyed kid, learning how to say "thank you" and "please" in Russian, visiting Moscow University, going to the ballet at the famous Bolshoi Theater, and watching the changing of the guard at Buckingham Palace in London.

Despite a minor foot injury, she set a new American record in the 80-meter hurdles at Braunschweig, Germany. That year too she had competed in the Caribbean Games in Jamaica and in an international meet in Toronto, Canada. Tammie's record and acclaim were building fast. Her father, a lab technician at the National Institute of Health in Bethesda, Maryland, her mother, and her three brothers and a sister were proud of her.

At the Millrose Games that February in New York, she beat the great German Olympic star Jutte Heine in the 50-yard dash and was again runner-up to Willye B. White and Jennifer Wingerson of Canada to become national indoor champion of the 50-yard dash.

In the 1964 outdoor nationals at Hanford, California, Debbie Thompson lost by inches both the girls' 50- and 75-yard dashes to speedy Lynda Bradshaw of Oakland, California, although in a trial heat of the race Debbie had set a record. But her big day was to come at the Olympic trials at Randalls Island in New York City.

On the basis of form and experience, Debbie Thompson was not supposed to make the Olympic team and certainly not expected to qualify in the 200 meters. When she ran fifth in the 100-meter finals and was eliminated, everyone congratulated her on her fine showing and remarked upon her great future promise. In the 200 meters she competed against Vivian Brown, a veteran runner of this distance who in 1962 had been clocked in the time of 24.1 seconds in the 220-yard dash, eclipsing the 27-year-old record of the controversial Stella Walsh, and swift and powerful Edith McGuire, who had won the 220-yard national championship and had beaten the Russians in the 200 meters only a month before. She also faced Shirley Wilson of the Compton Track Club, who had beaten her in the trial heat, and Diane Wilson of the Los Angeles Mercurrettes, who had been clocked in better than Olympic standard time.

The finals of the 200 meters were the next-to-last event in the competition. The Frederick team had suffered a hard-to-take defeat when Tammie, who had been second among the leaders in the 80-meter hurdles in the first day's trials with a time of 11 seconds, hit the last hurdle in the final race and slowed down to 11.3 seconds, coming in fourth, just out of the running.

The skies began to cloud. There were many unanswered questions about Debbie. She was so young and immature. Did she have the stamina for the longest and most grueling of the sprints?

Debbie got off to a slow start. She was trailing the field at the end of the first 50 or 60 yards; it looked like it was all over. Then she edged past Shirley Wilson, then Diana Wilson. Edith McGuire and Vivian Brown stayed in the lead, and it seemed certain that they would finish first and second, but at the last stride Debbie made a tremendous lunge for the tape and won literally by a neck. It took 30 minutes to examine the photograph made by the Bulova timer to determine the winner of second place. Both she and Vivian Brown were clocked at 23.7 seconds, seven-tenths of a second under the required Olympic standard. When it was finally decided, Debbie had won her place on the Olympic team and brought fame and honor to Frederick and Maryland.

It is difficult to fathom the effect of the Olympic Games on a young runner. Competing with thousands of athletes from nearly 100 countries before 80,000 spectators is bound to produce some tension even in a seasoned veteran. For the 17-year-old girl from a small town it was like a first plunge into an icy lake. Debbie was eliminated in her trial heat in the 200 meters. She ran fourth behind Louise Black, the Australian star who won a bronze medal in the finals. This was the end of Debbie's first Olympic competition.

But before returning to Frederick she was to run in Japan. At the British Commonwealth Games in Osaka, she ran third leg on the winning U.S. 400-meter relay team. Here, once again, she was pitted against the Australian girl. This time, in her lap she outran her. With other members of the team she received a gold medal. The time was only three-tenths of a second off the world record.

On June 30, 1966, the AAU outdoor nationals were held at the Thomas

Johnson Stadium in Frederick, a tribute to Frederick, Jack Griffin, and the track-and-field club he coached. But the girl who had brought the first fame to Frederick was not there. Debbie Thompson had married.

Tammie Davis had gone to Tennessee State and returned to the Frederick meet to take third place in the 80-meter hurdles. Debbie was too poor to go to college, and although she undoubtedly was one of three or four of the nation's best American women sprinters, she had to drop out of competition.

The amateur club to which Debbie belonged, the Frederick Track and Field Club, deserves some attention if we are to begin to understand something about women's track athletics in the United States. Frederick is not a large town, about 30,000 people, and there are no obvious reasons why it should produce a larger number of talented track stars than any other town its size or larger. Yet the curious fact is that in the Olympic trials in 1964 a total of 18 girls from the Frederick Track and Field Club competed in the trials, while Baltimore, with a population 42 times as large, didn't have a single athlete entered in the trials. Indeed, the lopsidedness of representation in women's track-and-field athletics throughout the United States tells a great deal about the nation's failure to recognize the importance of this form of women's athletics and the role it plays in building a positive international image for the United States.

The Frederick Track and Field Club was the fruit of the dedication of its coach, Jack Griffin, to track athletics and to interracial understanding. For the 30 preteens and teenagers who made up his roster, this experience in good health and good citizenship will last the rest of their lives. But more than this, the whole town of Frederick shines brightly among the towns and cities of America.

Griffin coached the U.S. Olympic women's track team at the 1964 Tokyo Olympics and is now Frederick's assistant director of adult recreation. Debbie Thompson-Brown is now an athletic coach at Frederick High School. In February 1991 Debbie Thompson was inducted into Maryland's Sports Hall of Fame.

Other towns and cities stand out as good track-and-field towns or bad ones, depending on the effort of public or private forces to service the needs of the young girls in their communities. The Police Athletic League of New York (PAL) has encouraged teams for more than three decades. It produced great stars like Mae Faggs and Patricia Monsanto.

The Youth Foundation of Chicago has also cultivated outstanding competitors. Originally, this team represented the Catholic Youth Organization and competed under the name Chicago Comets. Bishop Bernard J. Shield of Chicago sponsored the team in an effort to provide wholesome recreation for hundreds of teenage girls on the sprawling South

Side of Chicago. He wanted to create athletic opportunities for young people who had few outlets for their youthful energy.

The Comets, as they were then known, have always been interracial and have contributed a number of outstanding stars to U.S. teams competing in Olympic Games, Pan-American Games, and dual meets between the United States and foreign countries. Its members included Olympic medal winners Mable Landry of the 1952 Olympic team, Willye B. White, and Barbara Jones.

The Cleveland Recreation Department has fostered girls' track teams with excellent results. It too is interracial and has produced international stars like Vivian Brown, a member of the 1960 and 1965 Olympic teams, and Sandra Knott and Eleanor Montgomery, 1964 Olympians.

Another interracial club which has had some of its members on American international teams is the Los Angeles Mercurrettes. Marilyn White, a sprinter, and Terrezene Brown, a high jumper, were on the 1964 U.S. women's Olympic team. Charlotte Cook, champion in the 440-yard dash and Barbara Farrell, who was coholder of the world record in the 100 meters, were on the 1967 U.S. women's team at the Pan-American Games in Canada.

American colleges are generally not involved in women's track-and-field athletics. There are a few exceptions—Tennessee State University, Tuskegee Institute, the University of Hawaii, and the University of California at Los Angeles have outstanding women's track-and-field programs.

A number of smaller independent track clubs have been formed and have sent contenders to AAU meets. The Detroit Track Club, the Central Jersey Track Club, the Ohio Track Club, the Delaware Track and Field Club, and the Long Island Mercurrettes are typical of these independent organizations.

The significant thing, however, is that in a country as big as the United States there are only a few oases of women's track and field to be found in a vast Sahara of indifference, and these few could scarcely exist were it not for the dedication of coaches like Jack Griffin and a few others who see the importance of the sport as a builder of finer American womanhood. It is fortunate that there are a few unselfish high school teachers who spot some speedy little girl in pigtails who they think ought to have a chance to prove herself and see that she gets that chance.

Indeed, if there is any magic to the constant preeminence of Tennessee State University in women's track and field, it has been due largely to these teachers who sent their best athletes to the summer program conducted for high school students. But make no mistake about it; women's track is still the stepchild of American sports.

It is a fact to be spoken of not as a boast but certainly with a reasonable pride that most of the medals in women's track and field won since 1948 have been won by black American women. Black women have been under-represented in other Olympic sports, especially swimming, tennis, golf, equestrian riding, and fencing. This has been due in part to the fact that participation in these events requires expensive equipment and access to exclusive facilities (country clubs, riding academies, and swimming pools) that blacks are often not allowed to join or do not have the money for memberships. Imagine how good a swimmer, tennis player, or golfer Wilma Rudolph or any of a score of other black women might have been, given their natural athletic ability, if they had been exposed to these sports.

Cheryl Toussaint

Cheryl Toussaint won a silver medal as a member of the U.S.A.'s 1972 1600-meter relay team at the Munich Olympiad. A graduate of New York University, she ran as a member of the Atoms Track Club in Brooklyn. She held the world record in the indoor 600-yard dash.

Kim Turner

Kim Turner won a silver medal in the 100-meter hurdles at the 1964 Tokyo Olympics.

Wyomia Tyus

Wyomia won the world's attention with her performance at two Olympics. She was born August 29, 1945, in Griffin, Georgia, and like several other female track stars, started athletic life as a high school basketball player but quickly changed to track when her athletic teachers noticed her speed. Wyomia Tyus is truly one of the most remarkable athletes ever to represent the United States. Before she was 18, she was touring Europe demonstrating her talent; before her 19th birthday, she was setting world records.

Wyomia, like Wilma Rudolph, was a Tennessee State Tigerbelle and was trained by Coach Ed Temple. She held world records in the 50-, 60-,

70-, and 100-yard dashes. She won Olympic gold medals in the 100 meters in the 1964 and 1968 Olympiads. At the 1964 Tokyo Olympics she won the 100 meters in a world record breaking time of 11.4 seconds, and she ran on the United States' 1600-meter relay team that won the silver medal that year.

Four years later, at the 1968 Olympic in Mexico City, she won two more medals and became the first female sprinter to win gold medals in consecutive Olympics. She set a new 100-meter world record of 11 seconds flat and then ran anchor on the United States' winning 400-meter relay team, which set an Olympic and world record of 42.8 seconds.

She dedicated her gold medals to John Carlos and Tommy Smith, two American athletes who had been expelled from the Olympic Village for raising clenched fists on the victory podium during an awards ceremony. There had been efforts to get American athletes to boycott the 1968 Olympics to protest the "oppression and injustice" inflicted on black Americans. The president of the U.S. Olympic Committee harshly criticized the athletes for their demonstration and said they had violated "the basic standards of good manners and sportsmanship."

Black athletes were also concerned about the International Olympic Committee's decision to lift the ban it had imposed four years earlier on South Africa because of its policy of apartheid. The IOC left the ban in place after 30 African nations and the Soviet Union announced they would not attend the games if South Africa participated. But though the IOC acted swiftly when individual athletes attempted to use the games as a forum to express dissatisfaction with their own countries, it could do little to prevent participating nations from making political statements in the world arena. A headline on an article in the *Amateur Athlete* in August 1966 asked: "Who Needs the Russians?"

It was a signal of a serious breach in international sports competition between countries behind the Iron Curtain and the United States. After seven consecutive dual track-and-field meets between the U.S. and USSR, the Russians had abruptly canceled the eighth meet, scheduled for Los Angeles at the end of July 1966. The Russians were protesting the United States' involvement in the Vietnam War. Poland followed suit, and a hurriedly arranged dual meet between the Soviet Union and Poland was organized and scheduled to be held in Minsk, Russia. Meanwhile, an All-American Invitational was sanctioned by the AAU to be held in Los Angeles following the outdoor nationals at Frederick, Maryland.

The air was filled with recriminations. The Russians were "chicken," it was claimed. A staff writer for the *Los Angeles Times*, Shavenau Glick, wrote: "It is all speculative, of course, but the meaning is clear. The U.S.A. team, which was upset in Kiev last year, has come a long way, too far for the Soviets to match." Another article, in the *Amateur Athlete,* compared

Wyomia Tyus stands in a drenching rain as she listens to "The Star Spangled Banner" and receives her gold medal for winning the 100-meter dash at the 1968 Olympics in Mexico City, Mexico. Tyus' teammate, Barbara Ferrell, left, won the silver medal and Poland's Irene Szewinski won the bronze. AP/Wide World photo.

the records and distances set in the two meets and concluded that the Russians would have been beaten. The brouhaha among the Russians, the Americans, and the Poles cast a cloud over international sports competition; it gave support to the assertion that international sports competition is "war in another form."

There was now no longer any question of the truth of this assertion. All countries put their best foot forward by exploiting the skills of their outstanding athletes. Black Olympic winners have been the most valuable exhibit of the United States, especially in the developing countries of Africa. The State Department has missed no opportunity to exploit them by putting them on the world stage as spokespersons for America. That is why Edith McGuire and Wyomia Tyus were in Massawa, Ethiopia, when it was 100 degrees in the shade in August 1966. They were the United States' Exhibit A in a State Department–sponsored goodwill tour of African nations. Ambassador Korry made good use of them.

At Prince Makonnen Secondary School in Asmara, they met with 350 schoolteachers, newspaper editors, and about 100 children to whom they demonstrated the fundamentals of starting, running, baton passing, and other track basics. They toured the Ethiopian naval base and attended a formal banquet given by the base's commanding officer. They rode along a narrow road between Asmara and Massawa with its hairpin turns on a roller coaster–like ride while they looked over the sharp escarpments of scenic valleys hundreds of feet below.

They reached Addis Ababa in a blinding rain, put on several quick demonstrations at the Haile Selassie Stadium, and had their pictures taken with Ato Yidnekachev Tesema, director-general of the Ethiopian Sports Federation, and Colonel Bekele Gizaw, general sports manager of the Imperial Ethiopian Bodyguard. At a reception in the home of the assistant information officer of the U.S. Information Service, Lieutenant Abebe Bikkila, twice winner of the Olympic marathon, and Sergeant Mamo Wilde, another Ethiopian Olympic gold-medal winner, were there to greet the Americans. Ambassador Korry, in a State Department communique, wrote: "Perhaps the most impressed people at the reception were the girls invited from the Ethiopian YWCA. To them, Miss Tyus and Miss McGuire were a great inspiration who personified the freedom from reticence to which these young Ethiopian athletes aspire."

This was Edith's last track tour. She had graduated and would soon take a position with the Job Corps in Detroit. The year 1966 had gone pretty much her way. At Albuquerque, New Mexico, in the AAU indoor nationals she had run second to Wyomia in the 60-yard dash, trailed by the rising young runner Norma Harris. At the national outdoor meet in Frederick, Maryland, she had helped Tennessee State win the meet by running second to Wyomia in the 100-yard dash, third to Wyomia in the 220-yard dash, and sharing with Wyomia and two teammates a place on the winning 440-yard relay.

The competition had been fast but without any surprises. A new girl from California, Barbara Ferrell of the Los Angeles Mercurrettes, was an improving young runner on the cusp of making her mark in track history. In mid–July, at the All-American International in Los Angeles, Barbara ran first in the 100 meters in the rather slow time of 11.6 seconds. Wyomia and Edith finished second and third in 11.7 seconds, and in the 200 meters Edith won, but Barbara ran second to Wyomia's third. This was an upset. The following week, at the Los Angeles, Wyomia came back to win the 100 meters in 11.5 seconds; Barbara was second and Edith third. In the 200 meters Edith ran first, Barbara was second, and Wyomia was edged out of third place by Jennifer Lamy of Australia and finished fourth. Perhaps the Tennessee girls were getting tired. It proved, nevertheless, that gold medals or no gold medals, they could be beaten now and again. The title "world's fastest woman" was never meant to last for long.

In Oakland, California, in March 1967, Wyomia defended her 60-yard title, defeating Barbara Ferrell by inches. Wyomia now had three things on her mind, in this order: a black widow spider, Irena Kirszenstein, and

Barbara Ferrell. After the indoor nationals her trainer noticed something that looked like a burn on her ankle. An ointment was applied, but it did no good. Then the burn became a blister, and a doctor lanced it and applied more ointment, still without beneficial effect. Finally a second doctor examined the wound and diagnosed it as the bite of a black widow spider. She was out of training until three weeks before the outdoor nationals. Then, shortly before the meet, she had trouble with her leg again and couldn't train for three more days. Two crucial meets were ahead of her, the outdoor national and the meet for the trials for the Pan-American Games to be held in Winnipeg, Canada, in August.

At the outdoor nationals, Barbara Ferrell won the 100 meters and matched the world record of 11.1 seconds in doing so. Now, with Irena Kirszenstein, Ewa Klobukowska, and Wyomia she was coholder of the world record. Wyomia could run only third behind one of the younger teammates, Diana Wilson. In the 200 meters Diana won in the excellent time of 23.6 seconds. Barbara Ferrell was second and Wyomia third. She was not entered in the 800-meter medley relay.

Meanwhile, before the Pan-American Games, the U.S–British Commonwealth Games were held in Los Angeles. The 100 meters was anyone's race. An Australian girl, Diane Burge, came in first; a Canadian girl, Irena Piotrowski, edged out Barbara Ferrell for second; and Wyomia was fourth. It was something like the disappointing defeats in Moscow in 1963.

In between the Los Angeles meet and the Pan-American Games in Winnipeg, Wyomia spent the time getting in condition. She came back to form to win the 200 meters at Winnipeg. Then she went to Montreal to participate in a meet between teams representing the Americans in Europe. Officially, the Poles have broken off sports relations with the United States in 1966, but athletes were never impressed with cold-war politics.

In Montreal the Poles ran against the Americans. More important, Irena Kirszenstein was placed against Wyomia Tyus and Barbara Ferrell, three world record holders in a single race. It was August 20, 1967. Here was a perfect mirror on the wall to reflect the fastest of them all. Wyomia was first in 11.3 seconds, two-tenths of a second off the world record; Irena was second, a neck away, also in 11.3 seconds; Barbara was third, in 11.4 seconds. It was a blazing finish where attention to track fundamentals paid dividends. The *New York Times* said: "Miss Tyus leaned so hard to the tape to hold off her rivals during the finish that she fell and was stretched out on the track." "It was worth the win," said Wyomia.

In a column in the *New York Times* C.L. Sulzberger wrote: "When ancient Olympic Games were staged neither the concept of nation, state, nor amateurism existed and, when the idea was revived three generations ago there were few professionals in the sporting world. The thought that the flag followed the scoreboard was inconceivable." And writing in the

Amateur Athlete in 1961, Avery Brundage, then president of the International Olympic Committee, said: "Thus the Olympic Movement in these materialistic days in which we live carries the seeds of its own destruction even more than it did 2400 years ago, when Greek philosophers exclaimed against subsidization, the proselytizing, the excesses, the commercialization and other abuses that corrupted the ancient games. And steps must be taken to preserve its purity."

But it is no longer possible to ignore the fact that international sports have become inextricably involved with international politics. The Russians know this well. As early as 1958, in Moscow, Soviet newspapermen questioned America's black athletes about racial inequality and justice in the United States, attempting to exploit America's racial problems.

Victory for a national team has become a matter of national honor "more important," as the English miler Christopher Chataway wrote, "to national prestige than devaluation of the state of the armed forces."

The Soviet journal *Theory and Practice of Physical Culture* commented after the Tokyo Olympiad: "To the failures of U.S. policy in international affair, to the loss of its influence in several Asian, African and Latin-American countries have been added the defeats of American sportsmen in the international arena."

And Eastern-Bloc countries, especially the Soviet Union, no longer attempt to obscure the fact that they subsidize their Olympic athletes in an effort to garner the worldwide prestige that winning athletes gain for their countries. In Seoul, Korea, in 1988, Marat Gramov, a Soviet sports official, announced not only that the Soviet Union paid athletes and provided for most of their financial needs but that winning athletes were paid additional stipends ranging from 3,000 to 19,000 rubles.

With the AAU decision to soften its position on allowing athletes to earn income by endorsing products, U.S. Olympic participants for the first time are finding it possible to make money and compete more equally with athletes from other countries who receive the full support of their sponsoring nations. But many of the earlier American stars may have risen to even further accomplishments had it not been for these rules.

As Mrs. Marie Tyus, Wyomia Tyus' mother, said:

> I told the welfare, "I just can't make it." And they said, "Well, you ought to have plenty of money now." I said, "Why am I gonna have plenty of money now? I can't even hardly live." They say, "What about all that your daughter did?" I said, "My daughter don't get paid for that. Don't get it wrong now. My daughter don't get money for that." But I can't make some of these people believe that.

In 1969 Wyomia retired from amateur athletics. "After the Olympics I didn't even run across the street," she said. But four years later Wyomia was running again. She married and moved to Los Angeles in 1969 and after the birth of her daughter, Simone, decided to compete in national competition.

The International Track Association had been formed, and it paid athletes to run. In 1973, after four years of retirement, she won 8 of 18 races and in 1974 won 23 races on the tour. "The money was terrible," she said. "I think you got $600 for winning, and a little more if you set a world record."

Mabel Walker

Mabel Walker was a member of the U.S. team at the 1948 London Olympics. A high jumper and sprinter, she competed in the high jump but won no medal.

Marilyn White

Marilyn White ran on the U.S.A.'s second-place 400-meter relay team at the 1964 Tokyo Olympiad and won a bronze medal in the 100-meter dash.

Willye B. White

Citizens of Greenwood, Mississippi, will learn here for the first time that Willye Bertha White is possibly their most traveled native daughter. By the age of 29, she had traveled to Melbourne, Australia; Moscow, Russia; Warsaw, Poland; Budapest, Hungary; Karlsruhe and Stuttgart, Germany; Athens, Greece; London, England; Rome, Italy; Sao Paulo, Brazil; Tokyo, Japan; Winnipeg, Canada; Tel Aviv, Israel; and Mexico City, Mexico. In Tel Aviv in May 1966 Willye participated in the HOPAL Games. There she won the long jump and the 100 meters. And she traveled to more than a score of cities all over the United States to participate in international and national track-and-field meets.

Willye White is the daughter of Willie and Johnnie White. She changed the *i* to *y* in her name to stop being mistaken for a boy, but it infuriated her to have people change the pronunciation. Her father was a disabled World War II veteran. She was raised by her maternal grandparents and went to a segregated elementary school in Greenwood. There were four other White children growing up in Mississippi and Texas, but she was the oldest.

In 1950, when she was 10 years old and in elementary school, she tried out for the varsity track team, the high school team, and outran all the older girls. As Willye put it: "My cousin was on the track team and asked me to come out with her. I asked, 'What do you have to do?' and she said, 'All you do is run.' So I went out and beat everybody."

She made the team and competed in the area championship meets for all the black high schools in the area, the Big A meets. From 1953 to 1956, she led her high school to victory. Each of these years she won the 50-yard dash, the 50-yard hurdles, the 75-yard dash, the running broad jump, and she anchored the winning 300-yard relay team. She was a one-girl track team.

The summer of 1956 was a time when things happened beyond all of her expectations. Recommended by her high school coach, she was selected to attend Tennessee State University's summer track-and-field training program. After the program she won a place on the Tennessee team and went with it to compete in Philadelphia, at the national AAU meet. It was her first national track meet. For the 17-year-old this was to be the end of a wonderful summer of track athletics. Later she would have the opportunity to gain more experience. But Willye White began to demonstrate her outstanding ability then. She broad-jumped 18 feet, 6 inches to set a new American record in the girls' division.

On the next day, in women's competition, she finished second behind Margaret Matthews. Since her jumping exceeded the qualifying mark for Olympic competition, she was taken the following week to Washington, D.C., for the Olympic trials. When the trials were over, Margaret Matthews had set a new American record of 19 feet, 9½ inches, and Willye White had placed second, less than 6 inches behind. She had won a place on the Olympic team and was Melbourne-bound.

The hopes of the United States in women's running broad jump depended upon the performance of a 19-year-old girl who came from an Atlanta slum and a 17-year-old girl who was a Sunday school teacher in Greenwood, Mississippi, and whose auburn hair won her the nickname "Red." For both of them it was the biggest track meet of their lives, jumping in competition with seasoned veterans of many meets before a crowd of more than 100,000 excited spectators.

Great athletes never offer alibis—unless, of course, they are injured. Margaret Matthews never did, and neither did Willye White. Sometimes they had good days, at other times bad ones.

In Melbourne Margaret failed to qualify in the broad jump. Now it was up to Willye White. She qualified. In the final competition her best jump was 19 feet, 11 ½ inches, enough to win a second-place silver medal and set a new American citizen's record, passing that of Margaret Matthews. With a single jump, Willye White had leaped to fame.

Athletic competition follows the rule of ancient kings. The champion may never tire or show a sign of weakness. Always there is a challenger preparing ruthlessly to seize the victor's crown. This was the story of Willye White and Margaret Matthews for the next three years, with now and again a third teammate, Anna Lois Smith of Atlanta, waiting to catch both of them in a weak moment.

After Melbourne, Willye and Margaret returned to Tennessee State. In 1957 Willye won the broad jump in the girls' division at the national outdoor AAU meet, setting a new record, but in the women's division competition she was injured. A photographer at the end of the pit was trying to get a close-up action shot. Before she knew it, she had pulled a hamstring muscle while trying to avoid crashing into the cameraman. It ended her jumping that day, and her best previous jump left her in third place. The broad jump title in the women's division was won by Margaret, with Anna Lois Smith in second place.

In 1958 Margaret set a new American record by jumping 20 feet, 1 inch—the first time an American woman had broken the 20-foot barrier.

But Willye countered within days, jumping 20 feet, 2½ inches in Warsaw. This new record lasted only two days; Margaret jumped 20 feet, 3½ inches in Budapest.

Willye came back strong for the 1960 Olympic trials but did not perform as well in Rome.

> If someone had walked up to me in 1960 and said, "You won't win a gold medal in Rome," I would have shot him. In the Olympic trials I took one jump and jumped twenty feet, five inches, which then was good because only one woman had jumped twenty feet. Again, my leg hurt, but I was coming along fine. In dual meets we had that summer I jumped twenty feet, five inches six times, which meant I had consistency. So I was ready for Rome. I kept on training and was overtrained. I was overconfident, too, and this is as bad as no confidence. In Rome, I was the first one to jump and I had no excitement and no butterflies—and that was bad.

It was bad, indeed. Vera Krepkina of Russia won the gold medal in the event with a jump of 20 feet, 10¾ inches; Willye White finished in sixteenth place. Her American teammate, Anna Lois Smith, failed to qualify.

No one who has not participated in an Olympic meet can hope to understand the vagaries of athletic competition. There is no other athletic competition quite like it. Athletes from scores of nations contend with each other before thousands of spectators. Weather, track conditions, personal problems—a hundred variants of these—all weigh upon the competition, feed the athletes fears.

Like malaria, Olympic fever makes the athlete hot, then cold. Like sanity and madness, there is a thin line in the Olympics between victory and defeat. At Melbourne a 17-year-old, unsophisticated Mississippi girl won a silver medal; four years later she was not even in contention.

In order to gauge Willye White's performance, consider what happened to Mary Rand of England. In 1964 at Tokyo, Miss Rand set a new world record of 22 feet, 2¼ inches; in 1960 at Rome, she fouled out on all three of her jumps.

Between 1959 and 1960, things had changed for Willye. She left Tennessee State and went to Chicago where she hoped to settle down and study nursing. She had joined the track team of Mayor Daley, the Youth Foundation, in Chicago and had competed in the 1960 Olympic trials in Abilene, Texas, winning the event and to her great joy, breaking the record Margaret made at Budapest. But then came the debacle in Rome. She came back to Chicago and tried to enter nursing school.

Having been a member of two U.S. Olympic teams was not an advantage; it was a handicap. Willye told what happened:

> I was unable to get in school because I had been a member of the Olympic teams. This is when I tried to get into a nursing school to become a professional nurse. The lady I applied to felt that if I started school, I would think that I was more than the other kids. I couldn't convince her that all I wanted to do was to go to school. The lady had never met me before in her life, and I walked in and talked to her and she told me, "You think you are more than the other kids," and I said, "I do not." Then she asked, "What are you going to do about running?" She said, "If I had the opportunity to run all around the world, I wouldn't stop to become a nurse."

With limited funds and no scholarship, Willye went to the Chicago Board of Education School of Nursing and became a practical nurse, but she did not stop "running all around the world."

In 1961 she was on the U.S. team which toured Europe. It was coached by Marian Armstrong-Perkins (Morgan) and included Wilma Rudolph, Vivian Brown, Jo Ann Terry, Edith McGuire of Tennessee State, and Ernestine Pollard of Chicago's Youth Foundation.

In Moscow, Willye placed second behind Tatanya Schelkanova, who jumped 21 feet, 11 inches for a new world record, but Willye's jump of 20 feet, 11½ inches was 1 inch better than the jump that had won the gold medal at the Olympics in Rome the year before. It set a new American record that lasted just two days, for at Karlsruhe, Germany, Willye bettered her own mark and became the first American girl to jump over 21 feet (21 feet, ¼ inch). This record lasted five days until the team got to London. Here Willye beat her mark again. She jumped 21 feet, ¾ inch, just 1¼ inch off the world record. This was the girl who had finished sixteenth in the Rome Olympics.

Willye's 1961 performance as a broad jumper clouded her equally brilliant record that year as a sprinter. In the Moscow meet she ran first leg on the 400-meter U.S. relay team with Ernestine Pollard, Vivian Brown, and Wilma Rudolph. The team ran the relay in 44.3 seconds, clipping a tenth of a second off the Olympic record made at Rome and setting a new world record. At Stuttgart, Germany, Wilma Rudolph set a new world record of 11.2 seconds in the 100 meters, but it was Willye, nipping at her heels, who pushed her to the tape, winning second place in a time that equaled the old world record. In London, because Wilma was sick and exhausted, Willye paced the American team to victory in the dual meet with England The *New York Times* reported: "The top United States woman star today was Willye White of Chicago. Last night she had taken the broad jump with a tremendous 21 foot one-and-three-quarter inches effort. This afternoon she won the 100-yard dash in 0:10.9 seconds and handed over a two-yard lead in the first leg of the relay." At 22, Willye ranked with Wilma Rudolph among the finest women athletes in the world.

One of the ironies of amateur athletics in the United States is that we expect so much out of athletes and invest so little in their training and development. With a single voice the great mass of American people cheer the great victories of track stars in the Olympics and in dual meets with Russia and other countries. They are "our girls." But let their performance be less than hoped for, and a shrill, fickle chorus of American press and public can be heard saying "girls are cream puffs, the girls won't train." What the public does not know is how difficult it is for the American woman athlete to find opportunities for training. Willye White is a case in point.

When Willye left Tennessee State and went to Chicago, she was on her own in her athletic career. Although affiliated with the Youth Foundation, she had no one to coach her in broad jumping, little time for systematic training, and limited opportunity for competition. Little wonder that her 1962 performance fell below that of 1961. It was not that Willye did not win. She was still the best woman broad jumper in the United States. It was that she did not better her 1961 record. She won both the indoor and outdoor AAU broad jump championships in 1962 and was also indoor champion in the 50-yard dash. She was first in the broad jump in the Poland–United States dual meet and placed second, behind Tatanya Schelkanova, in the Soviet Union–United States meet. But her best jump in competition was only 20 feet, 3½ inches, almost a foot behind her best leap in 1961.

In 1963 she fell even further behind. She placed third in the AAU national outdoor meet, and now more than two feet behind her best 1961 jump. She had done 11 inches better seven years before at Melbourne when she was just 17. But even with this deterioration of her athletic condition, she still won the American championship in the 50-yard dash and set a new Pan-American Games record with a jump of 20 feet, 2 inches.

It is enlightening to compare Willye's development with that of her chief Russian rival, Tatanya Schelkanova. At this time in the Soviet Union athletes chosen for the national team were paid the most careful attention by their coaches over a long preparatory period, whereas the American team had barely a month to prepare for grueling competition. In Russia there was year-round training and competition for the best athletes. Earning a living and personal problems were not allowed to interfere with training. In this environment, Russian athletes made steady progress. Schelkanova, for example, in 1961 set a world record with a jump only 1 1/4 inches better than Willye's best jump that year. In 1962 she set a new world record of 21 feet, 5 inches to compare with Willye's best effort in 1962 of 20 feet, 3 1/2 inches. The performance gaps between the athletes had grown from slightly more than an inch to over a foot in a year.

With Willye, training was catch-as-catch-can before or after a full day's work and on weekends. Sound training and frequent competition is what makes a champion. Willye knew as well as anyone the importance of good conditioning, but she couldn't afford to take time off from her job to reach peak condition or to compete in a large number of track meets. No wonder that in competition with better-trained athletes American women have been at a disadvantage. As the *New York Times* reported in July of 1964, "In the United States, women's track is a step-child, so it will be no surprise if the Soviet women sweep their 10 events here."

It wasn't quite that way. Willye did lose to Schelkanova. The Russian girl, still developing, broke her own world record with a leap of 21 feet, 10 1/4 inches, but Willye, in second place, was only 2 1/2 inches behind at 21 feet, 7 3/4 inches. Because this jump was aided by the wind, it was not allowed to stand as a record, but another of her jumps, 21 feet, 6 inches, was declared a new American record. With Willye running the first leg, the American girls won the 400-meter relay in a time only one-tenth of a second off the world record, the record Willye had helped make in Moscow in 1961. And she won the 100 meters, the 200 meters, and the high jump. Not exactly a Soviet sweep, as predicted by the *New York Times*.

Soon after the dual meet with the Soviet Union, Willye, who had already recaptured her AAU indoor and outdoor broad jump titles, participated in the trials for the 1964 Olympics. She placed first in the broad jump with a leap of 21 feet, 4 inches, with a relative newcomer, Martha Watson of the Long Beach Comets Track and Field Club, second, jumping

21 feet, 3 inches. Jo Ann Terry, a veteran of the Tennessee State track team and now an Indianapolis schoolteacher, was third. These three athletes represented the United States in the broad jump at Tokyo.

When Willye White and Earlene Brown were chosen to represent the United States at the Tokyo Olympiad, sports history was made. Both of them had won this honor twice before; they competed at Melbourne and at Rome. No other American woman athlete had participated in three Olympic competitions except Mae Faggs.

The broad jumpers competed in Tokyo's National Stadium before a capacity crowd of 72,000. It was gusty and rainy. Martha Watson and Jo Ann Terry failed to qualify. Willye White had the fourth best jump in the qualifying competition—20 feet, 8½ inches. In the finals her best jump was only 19 feet, 11 inches, placing her twelfth in the competition. It was a painful disappointment. But even in her hour of defeat she came home with a silver medal for running the first leg on the American 400-meter relay team.

The big question is "What made Willye jump?" Like Margaret Matthews, she was never relaxed. She said that while tension paralyzes other athletes, she had to work herself up to a state of high excitement to perform at her best. If there were no butterflies in her stomach at the time of competition, she didn't feel right. The fact was that Willye was either very, very good or very, very bad. She was always fighting a private war with herself, and no one except Willye knew how to win the war.

In Tokyo, in Rome, it is possible that Willye wanted to win too badly. Even in Chicago two months before the event she was worrying about the difference a crushed-clay runway would make in her jumping style. She was accustomed to jumping on a rubberized or asphalt surface. And she was eating, sleeping, and thinking scores of facts she knew about her competitors. Weeks before the Olympic contest, she recognized Mary Rand of England as the girl she had to beat. The English girl, who had fouled out in Rome, was crowned Olympic champion and established the unprecedented world record of 22 feet, ½ inch. At the turn of the century, a jump of this distance would have won an Olympic crown for a man.

Willye spoke often about the special demands placed upon women athletes:

> It is pretty difficult being all female, you know, because you are out there on the track and you're in all that dirt and grime and grit doing the same things the boys are doing, and you don't carry yourself as feminine as some girls would. You're not as dainty as they are because most times your feet hurt, you have sore muscles, and it's pretty difficult to be all woman out on the track. This is something that you just can't be; you gotta let yourself go, whereas the average woman is constantly fixing her makeup or combing her hair and trying to look pretty. Well, when you're

out on the track with makeup on and you start sweating, it smears; and that makes you look worse. So what you do is your hard work and you look ugly out on the track and after the track meet is over you come back, fix yourself up, and then you're a pretty lady.

Dianne Williams

Dianne Williams, a sprinter, was a member of the U.S.A.'s 1984 Olympic team. She ran in the 100 meters but did not distinguish herself.

Lucinda Williams

The third runner on the 1960 Olympic relay team with Wilma Rudolph, Barbara Jones, and Martha B. Hudson was Lucinda Williams. She came from Bloomingdale, Georgia. They called her Lady Dancer. She always looked as if she had "just come off an ironing board" one of her friends said. She was neat, immaculate, full of spirit. On the Rome relay team she set a blistering pace. Lucinda had been a member of the Tigerbelle team at Ponca City in 1955 and had run on the U.S. relay team which took third place at Melbourne. Like Barbara Jones, she had beaten the Russians in the 200 meters, in Moscow in 1958 and Philadelphia in 1959.

At the Pan-American Games in Chicago in 1959, with 32 countries competing, she had won the 100- and 200-meter races, and had run anchor on the winning 400-meter relay team, winning three gold medals.

Lillian Young

Lillian Young competed in the 80-meter hurdles in 1948 but won no medal.

Appendix:
Sex, Chromosomes, and Gold Medals

Art critics have debated for centuries whether the model for Leonardo da Vinci's *Mona Lisa* was a man, but the controversy has done nothing to diminish the appreciation of the classic portrait painted by the Italian master.

The question of sex, however, has become a significant issue in women's track and field. Wilma Rudolph, Jackie Joyner-Kersee, and Florence Griffith-Joyner aside, probably the best-known woman athlete in the United States, if indeed she was a woman was not an American at all but a Polish athlete named Stella Walasiewicz. We will discuss the strange and unsettling circumstances of Stella Walasiewicz's sexuality shortly, but first it is important to review the Polish athlete's amazing field career. Walasiewicz ran for Poland and was women's 100-meter champion. In 1936, Walasiewicz again ran for Poland and took second place in the 100 meters behind Helen Stephens of the United States. Later, as a naturalized American citizen with an Americanized last name, Stella Walsh became a national champion at AAU track-and-field meets 37 times. An all-around athlete, Walsh won the outdoor women's 200-meter run 9 times and was national outdoor champion in the long jump 10 times. Walsh competed for nearly 30 years and ran for the last time in 1958 at the age of 47.

For several generations of American women athletes, Stella Walsh was the whetstone against which they sharpened their track-and-field skills. For 20 years of competition, during which Walsh set more than 87 national and world records, she seesawed back and forth with ambitious young runners and jumpers who were attempting to capture her crown.

Many of these newcomers were black athletes like Louise Stokes of Malden, Massachusetts, and Tidye Pickett, the hurdler from Chicago, the first two black women to make a U.S. Olympic team (1932). Other fierce competitors of Stella Walsh included Mabel Landry of Chicago, the broad jumper, and Alice Coachman and Nell Jackson of Tuskegee Institute. All of them made the 1948 U.S. Olympic team.

The story of Stella Walsh's athletic career is perhaps one of the strangest in the chronicles of women's track and field, and it casts a cloud of questions over the record books. It is part of the protracted controversy about the sexuality of some female athletes.

There had been frequent insinuations and persistent rumors that Walsh was actually a man masquerading as a woman. One Polish journalist accused Walsh of being a man, and in response, German Olympic officials in 1936 issued a statement asserting that they had given Walsh a thorough physical examination and determined that the Polish star was indeed a woman.

But 40 years later, on December 4, 1980, Stella Walsh was buying decorations for a Polish-American dance in a Cleveland, Ohio, discount store when an unfortunate twist of fate laid bare the bizarre truth of her sexuality. When she went to the store's parking lot, she was shot to death by gunmen who were attempting to hold up the store. An autopsy performed by the Cleveland Medical Examiner's office revealed that Stella Walsh had male sexual organs and biologically was a man.

Walsh had defeated some of the best women athletes in the world, set 11 world records, won AAU titles and two Olympic medals.

The question of an Olympic athlete's sexuality has been a controversial one ever since the ancient games. In ancient Greece, athletes paraded nude around the stadium before the games began. In 1968, the International Olympic Committee began screening tests to determine the chromosome composition of female athletes to "insure femininity of the competitors" and "establish equality among athletes."

The case of Stella Walsh was not decided on the basis of sophisticated biological examinations of chromosome balance. The medical examiner's report simply concluded that she had the gross anatomy of a male.

Had the gender-verification test, known medically as a "buccal smear," or the ancient "nude parade" been used in the 1930s, Stella Walsh might never have set her records, and women who finished second and third behind her may have won gold and silver medals.

It is historically ironic that with the exception of Stella Walsh, Alice Coachman won more national championships than any other woman, 26. She was national outdoor high jump champion for 10 straight years, 1939 through 1948, and outdoor 50-meter champion for 5 years, 1943 through 1947. Stella Walsh and Alice Coachman was one of the greatest athletes she ever competed against. Coachman and Walsh went back and forth in competition for national 100-meter championships. Walsh won it in 1943 and 1944, Coachman in 1945 and 1946.

The buccal smear, a microscopic examination of cells scraped from inside an athlete's cheek, is used to determine a person's chromosome pattern. In most instances, the female pattern is *xx* and the male pattern is *xy*. When IOC physicians discover what appears to be an abnormality, the athlete is subjected to a series of gynecological and clinical tests to determine if she is "feminine" enough to compete in Olympic competition.

Geneticists believe the incidence of chromosome defects ranges from one in 1,000 to one in 4,000. Some people born with indefiniteness in their sex organs and secondary sex characteristics may be treated medically or surgically at birth to produce as congruous a sexual identity as possible.

Eva Klobukowska, the Polish sprinter, was the first of about a dozen athletes to be banned from competition after the chromosome test was employed at the European Track and Field Championships in 1967. The International Olympic Committee's Medical Commission told Klobukowska the test disclosed irregularities in her chromosome balance, that subsequent clinical examinations indicated she had "male-like characteristics," and that she had been competing "unwittingly as a man." She was quoted as saying, "I know what I am and how I feel. . . . It's a dirty and stupid thing to do to me." She had won an Olympic gold medal and was world record holder in the 100-meter dash. But the IOC stripped her name from the official records, and the public recognition of her awards was taken away.

Some observers believe Klobukowska was treated unjustly, that the IOC's conclusion about the athlete's sexuality mirrored a primitive ignorance of the biological condition of athletes like her.

In addition to the revelations brought to light by Stella Walsh's autopsy, there is the case of Herman "Dora" Ratjen of Bremen, Germany. Ratjen confessed in 1957 that in the 1930s he had been forced to bind his genitals and pose as a woman by officials of the Nazi Youth Movement. In the 1936 Olympic Games in Berlin, the "Hitler Games," Ratjen qualified as a woman in the high jump finals and came in fourth. In 1938, still posing as a woman, he set a world high jump record at a national meet.

Because of their strength and masculine appearance, two famous Russian athletes, Tamara and Irina Press, were accused of being men. From 1959 to 1965 they won five gold medals and set 26 world records. In 1966, at the European Track and Field Championships, women competitors were required for the first time to undress for a "nude parade" before a panel of gynecologists. All 234 athletes, including Klobukowska, passed the examination, but several Eastern-bloc athletes, including Tamara and Irina Press, who were scheduled to compete, failed to appear. Many people believed that they did not appear because they would have failed the test. When the controversy over their sexuality continued, they stopped competing, returned to Russia, and dropped from public view. Irina Press had won the 1960 gold medal in the 100-meter hurdles, beating hurdler Carol Quinton of Great Britain by a tenth of a second. Tamara Press won the

1960 shot put, beating American Earlene Brown. Willye White, who had
set a world record at a U.S.-USSR meet in 1964 that had been broken
soon afterward by a Russian athlete whose femininity had been questioned,
said, "If she hadn't been a man, I would have been the world record
holder."

There have been other questions raised about athletes who competed
as women and later lived as men after winning prestigious medals. And
there have been instances in which female athletes have later changed their
sex through surgery. The IOC has characterized these athletes as "im-
posters" and charged that they had an unfair advantage over their competitors.

Since 1958, the IOC has screened all women competitors. The IOC
Medical Commission has said, "It would be unfair in a women's competition to allow athletes with abnormal chromosomes and with male-like
characteristics to compete." But the American College of Physicians and
the American College of Obstetricians and Gynecologists passed a resolu-
tion in 1988 urging abandonment of the chromosome test, calling it
"discriminatory" because men are not tested. They suggested that female
athletes be given only basic medical examinations by female doctors. The
two medical panels contend that the buccal smear test is inconclusive and
that regular physical examinations are simpler, more dignified, and more
pragmatic. But an editorial in the International Olympic Committee's
magazine supported the chromosome test: "The chromosome test in-
dicates quite definitely the sex of a person."

The *Journal of the American Medical Association* asked in an editorial,
"How often do competitors wittingly seek to deceive the IOC?" It said that
"genetic males" raised as females believe they are women. "We physicians
tell them so! To accuse such individuals of willful deception would be
churlish."

"It is imperative that this group of individuals not be discriminated
against," said Dr. Jean Wilson, an endocrinologist, in a 1968 letter to the
IOC, discussing what she believes to be the danger of the buccal smear test.
"It would be better for individual athletes to receive a competitive advantage than for the underlying diagnoses to be exposed in this cruel and
heartless manner."

Myron Genel, a pediatric endocrinologist and associate dean at Yale
University School of Medicine, is concerned about the philosophical im-
plications of the test as well. "What makes a woman?" Genel asked. "What
it comes down to is a question of femininity. Should it be left to a hand-
ful of people at the IOC, most of whom are men, to decide who is feminine enough to compete?" The IOC Medical Commission contends its aim
is not to issue ex cathedra decisions about who is a man and who is a
woman.

The records set by Walsh remain on the books, and no decision has yet been made by the IOC to strike Walsh's name and records from the official track-and-field registers.

The practice of issuing a "fem card" to all female Olympic contestants remains a controversial one. The IOC has pledged to find a more equitable method of handling this problem in the future.

Index